QUESTION & ANSWER
ENCYCLOPEDIA

The USA

This is a Parragon Publishing Book
This edition published in 2006

This edition was created by
Starry Dog Books

Parragon Publishing
Queen Street House
4 Queen Street
Bath, BA1 1HE
UK

ISBN 1-40547-655-9

Printed in China

Written by Nicola Barber, Jason Hook, Patricia Levy, Chis Oxlade and Sean
Sheehan

Illustrated by Sarah Crouch, Tim Mayer, and Victoria Webb

QUESTION AND ANSWER
ENCYCLOPEDIA
The USA

p

Contents

The Civil War

Presidents

Sporting Heroes

Great Americans

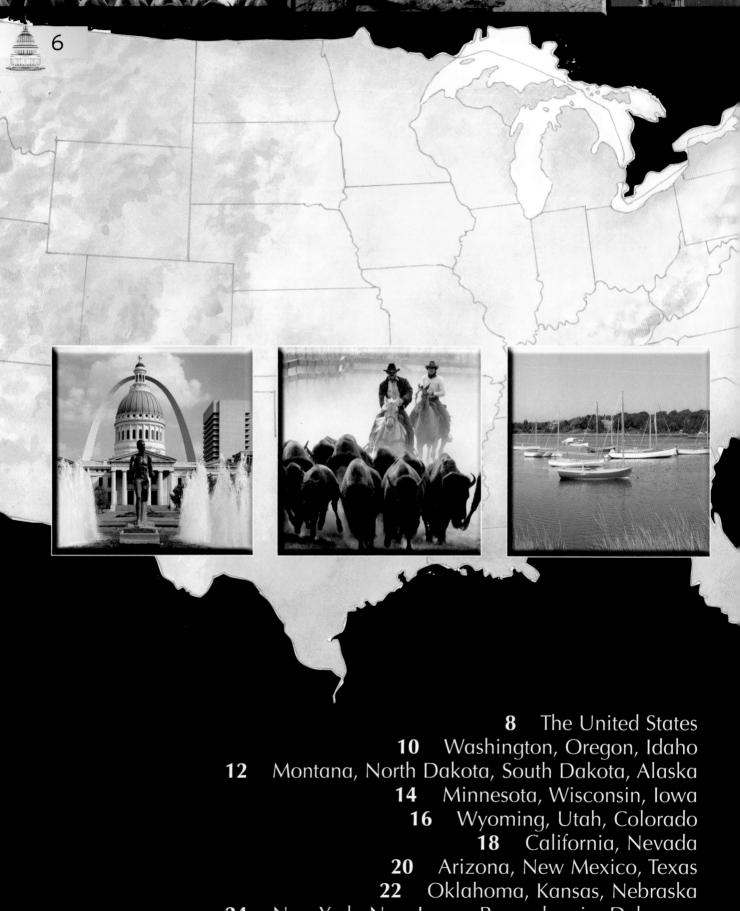

The 50 States

The United States

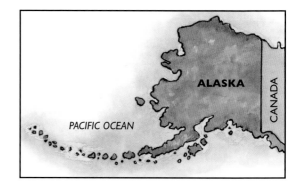

ALASKA

CANADA

PACIFIC OCEAN

The Capitol building and the Washington Monument in Washington, D.C.

CAPITAL FACTS

Area of District of Columbia:
61 sq miles (158 sq km)
Population: Washington D.C.
563,384

HAWAII

PACIFIC OCEAN

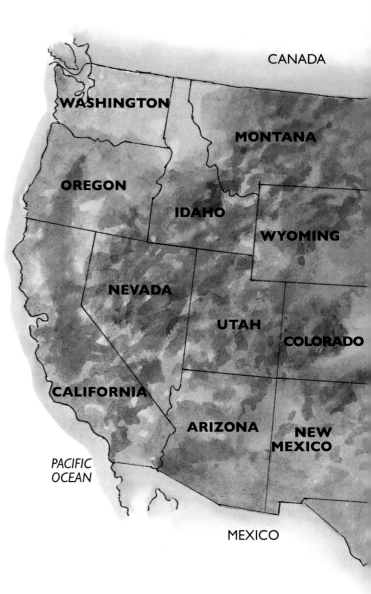

CANADA

WASHINGTON

MONTANA

OREGON

IDAHO

WYOMING

NEVADA

UTAH

COLORADO

CALIFORNIA

ARIZONA

NEW MEXICO

PACIFIC OCEAN

MEXICO

NB: Hawaii and Alaska are not shown at the same scale as the rest of the U.S.

U.S. FACTS

Area: 3,716,830 sq miles
(9,629,091 sq km)

Population: 293,027,571

Length of coastline:
12,373 miles (19,924 km)

Highest point:
Mt McKinley, Alaska
20,320 feet (6,194 meters)

Lowest point: Death Valley,
California –282 feet
(–86 meters)

NEW
HAMPSHIRE

VERMONT   MAINE

NEW
YORK

MASSACHUSETTS

MICHIGAN

NORTH
DAKOTA

MINNESOTA

WISCONSIN

RHODE
ISLAND

PENNSYLVANIA

CONNECTICUT

SOUTH
DAKOTA

NEW JERSEY

IOWA

OHIO

DELAWARE

NEBRASKA

INDIANA

MARYLAND

ILLINOIS

WEST
VIRGINIA

VIRGINIA

WASHINGTON, D.C.

KANSAS

MISSOURI

KENTUCKY

NORTH
CAROLINA

TENNESSEE

OKLAHOMA   ARKANSAS

SOUTH
CAROLINA

GEORGIA

ATLANTIC OCEAN

ALABAMA

TEXAS

MISSISSIPPI   FLORIDA

LOUISIANA

GULF OF MEXICO

**KEY to the maps of
the 50 states**
☐ National capital
(Washington, D.C.)
◼ State capitals
● Other main cities

Where does a phantom ship sail across a volcano?

In Crater Lake National Park, southwestern Oregon. In the crater of an extinct volcano, a lake has formed. It is surrounded by cliffs 500–2,000 ft (150–600 m) high, and at the southern end is a mass of lava, which looks like a ship under sail.

How did Idaho get its unusual shape?

On the map, Idaho is shaped like a platform boot with a large, almost square section in the south, but an odd north–south section. Idaho was created after the six states and one Canadian province that surround it had created their borders. It is a strip of land that no one else claimed. The surrounding settlers would have acted differently had they realized what a wealth of silver, zinc, lead, and lumber Idaho would eventually give up!

Where can you see salmon climbing a ladder?

The Columbia River in the state of Washington has been dammed in several places, and this makes it impossible for salmon to reach their breeding grounds. At Bonneville Dam, a special ladder has been built so the salmon can jump in stages up the height of the dam.

Who were the first Europeans to catch sight of Oregon?

Probably Spanish sailors in the 1500s. The headland of the Columbia River was given the name Cape Disappointment, because explorers thought the river mouth was only the entrance to a bay. In 1792, the river was discovered by Robert Gray, who named it after his ship, the *Columbia*.

Crater Lake is the second deepest lake in North America.

What lay dormant for 130 years until 1980?

The already grumbling volcano, Mount St. Helens. On May 18, 1980, this peak in the Cascade mountain range in Washington erupted after a severe earthquake opened a crack along its side. The side of the mountain blew out and debris, lava, and ash spread out in a 17 mile (27 km) arc, flattening forests in its path. Fifty-seven people were killed and the original height of the mountain—9,677 ft (2,950 m)—was reduced by 1,312 ft (400 m).

Where does a snake run into hell?

The Snake River runs through Idaho. It cuts through the Rocky Mountains in the west of the United States at Hell's Canyon. This is the deepest river gorge in North America at 7,900 ft (2,407 m). It is part of the Hell's Canyon Wilderness, a National Park.

How did the first families to cross the continent meet a disastrous end?

Marcus Whitman, his wife Narcissa, the Rev. Henry Spalding, and his wife made the first wagon train crossing to include women. They built a mission at Waiilatpu, and helped other families make the crossing after them. But in 1874, they and 12 other people were killed by Native Americans.

Why did Lewis and Clarke go up-river?

Lewis and Clarke were the two men chosen by President Thomas Jefferson in 1804 to explore the land west of the Mississippi River. They took a small party and followed the Missouri River to its source, crossed the continental divide, and then found and followed the Columbia River. Their expedition gave America its claim to the Oregon territories.

Which state is famous for its apples?

The area of Washington to the west of the Cascade mountain range has some of the thickest forests in the world. It is also one of the wettest areas in the U.S., and this makes the area good for growing produce. In fact, Washington grows more apples than any other state in the United States. East of the Cascade Range there is little rain and few trees.

Which Seattle-born businessman is mega-rich?

Bill Gates of the Microsoft Corporation. He made his first billion at the age of 31 after inventing the MS-DOS system and then Windows. Today he is one of the richest men in the world.

Washington

Oregon

Idaho

CANADA

Pacific Ocean

Seattle
Spokane
Olympia
WASHINGTON
Portland
Salem
OREGON
Boise
Idaho Falls
MONTANA
IDAHO
WYOMING
CALIFORNIA
NEVADA

Why is Montana named the Bonanza State?

Montana has many nicknames, including Big Sky Country, Land of the Shining Mountains, and the Treasure State. It is also called Bonanza, because of its wealth of natural resources. Montana has huge stretches of fertile soil suitable for growing wheat and grassland for grazing cattle. It also has valuable minerals and millions of acres of timber, particularly spruce, larch, and pine, which are all fast-growing and very good for commercial use.

"Calamity" Jane was born in Princeton, Missouri. She is said to have promised "calamity" to any man who tried to court her.

What was Custer's Last Stand?

In 1874, gold prospectors flooded into South Dakota, regardless of the understandably hostile Sioux whose land it was. General Custer was part of the force sent to protect the prospectors and drive the Cheyenne and the Lakota off the land meant for the Crow tribe. In 1876, disobeying orders, he led his troops into an ambush by 6,000 Native Americans at Little Big Horn. He and all 264 of his soldiers were killed. This event was named Custer's Last Stand.

Who was the real Calamity Jane?

She was born Martha Jane Canary, in 1852. She lived in Virginia City, Montana, and was a good horsewoman. Stories tell of how she fought Native Americans, wore men's clothes, and drank too much.

Cowboys are not just a thing of the past; in Montana these cowboys are rounding up a herd of young buffalo.

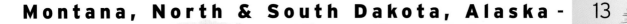

What are the Badlands?

An area of North and South Dakota where erosion has carved strange shapes out of the rock and there is no vegetation. Pioneers named it the Badlands because it was so difficult to cross. In places, underground lignite (brown coal) fires have melted the rock and created a mass of striking colors. The remains of saber-toothed tigers have been found there.

North Dakota

South Dakota

Montana

Where is "the richest hill on Earth"?

At Butte, Montana. In 1881, a prospector, Marcus Daly, who was searching for silver, found copper instead. The town of Butte grew up quickly and soon turned into a lawless place with bandits controlling the roads. Daly's Anaconda Company became one of the biggest mining companies in the world.

Where can you find the second longest mountain chain in the world?

In Montana, which is crossed by the Rocky Mountains. They begin far north of Montana in Alaska, cross Canada, and dominate the western third of the United States, but their main bulk is in Montana. Granite Peak is the highest mountain in the state at 12,799 ft (3,901 m).

Where would you find the world's tallest structure made by humans?

Surprisingly, not in New York City, but in North Dakota, where the KVLY-TV mast is 2,063 ft (619 m) high. It is supported by guy wires and would not stand up on its own.

Why is "big" an important word for Alaska?

When Alaska joined the Union, it increased the size of the U.S. by a fifth. It brought with it some big facts. It has 28,000 miles (44,800 km) of glaciers; the highest mountain in North America (Mount McKinley); the largest carnivorous land mammal (the Kodiak bear); and part of the longest navigable waterway in the world (the Yukon River).

Alaska

Pacific Ocean

Who created the famous cartoon called Peanuts?

Charles M. Schultz. He was born in Minneapolis, Minnesota, in 1922 and invented the cartoon strip Peanuts in 1950. It was originally named Li'l Folks, but has always included the beagle dog Snoopy and his owner Charlie Brown. It is the most successful cartoon strip in the world.

Why did Marion Morrison change names?

Marion became one of Iowa's most famous citizens, starring in films such as *Stagecoach* (1939), *True Grit* (1969), *The Alamo* (1960), and many more. He was in fact John Wayne, born in Winterset, Iowa, in 1907. He changed his name, for obvious reasons, in the 1930s. In 1979, he died of lung cancer.

How does Minnesota protect its wildlife?

Minnesota has vast resources of forest and was once a major logging center. Recently, Minnesota has set aside more land for wildlife preservation than any other state. In several areas where trees were cut down, the forest has been replanted.

Minnesota

WISCONSIN
1848
Wisconsin

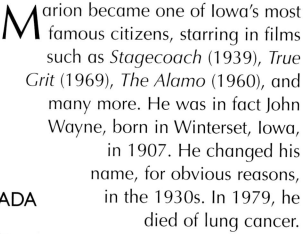

CANADA

Lake Superior

N. DAKOTA

Duluth

MICHIGAN

Lake Michigan

S. DAKOTA

MINNESOTA

St Paul
Minneapolis

WISCONSIN

Madison

Milwaukee

NEBRASKA

IOWA

ILLINOIS

OHIO

Des Moines

MISSOURI

IOWA
Iowa

Why was wheat from Iowa used to make bread in Moscow, Russia?

Iowa produces masses of grain—over a billion tons in some years. In the 1950s, the rest of the U.S. bought little of this harvest and Iowa farmers began to suffer. Then Soviet premier Khrushchev visited Iowa and set up a trade link between Iowa and Russia. The trade earned the state a huge annual revenue and it came to depend on it. In 1979, there was a trade embargo (ban) following the Afghanistan war, but the link was re-established in 1981.

What leisure activities do people enjoy in Wisconsin's great outdoors?

Hunting is a very popular sporting activity in Wisconsin, particularly for bear, game birds, and deer. The vast areas of lakeland offer fishing—especially for the curiously named muskellunge—and watersports of many kinds. In winter there are iceboat races on Lake Winnebago.

Who added his own bad name to the English language?

In 1950, Joseph McCarthy, the senator for Wisconsin, claimed he had a list of communists employed by the State Department. The Senate Committee for un-American activities began investigations into communist activity within government. Many people in the film industry were ruined by the investigations, although no accusations were ever proven. Finally, McCarthy went too far and accused President Eisenhower of being a communist. The word "McCarthyism" now means the persecution of innocent people with unproved charges.

Which is America's cheesiest state?

Wisconsin has been America's leading producer of milk since 1920, and today has about 3.35 million cows and calves. The first cheese factory was opened there in 1841, and Wisconsin cheese is internationally renowned. The state also has many creameries and butter factories.

How did a Gumm become a Garland?

Film star Judy Garland (1922–69) was born in Grand Rapids, Minnesota, although she didn't spend much of her time there. Her real name was Frances Gumm, and she worked as a child performer in her parents' singing act. Fame as a film star came after she was spotted by Louis B. Mayer of MGM studios.

John Wayne was world famous for acting the part of cowboys in Western films.

Where was the world's first national park created?

Yellowstone National Park, stretching across Wyoming, Idaho, and Montana. Established in 1872, it was the first protected area for wildlife in the world. Here you can see the geyser named Old Faithful, the hot springs, the Yellowstone Falls, rock formations, and herds of wild buffalo.

What is the Rainbow Bridge?

The Rainbow Bridge is the world's largest natural bridge, found in a national park in southeastern Utah. It is a salmon pink sandstone arch 290 ft (88 m) high and 275 ft (84 m) wide. Native Americans once considered it a sacred site. The first white men saw it in the 1800s.

Colorado

Utah

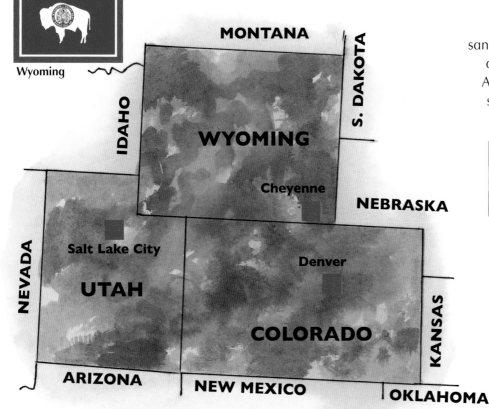

Wyoming

MONTANA

S. DAKOTA

IDAHO

WYOMING

Cheyenne

NEBRASKA

NEVADA

Salt Lake City

Denver

UTAH

COLORADO

KANSAS

ARIZONA

NEW MEXICO

OKLAHOMA

What do Esther, Spotted Tail, Robert, and John have in common?

They are all famous citizens of Wyoming, Utah, and Colorado. Wyoming's Esther Morris was an important figure in the women's suffrage movement; in 1870 she became the world's first woman to hold judicial office. Spotted Tail was a Wyoming Sioux chief who for a long time preserved his nation's territory and avoided war with white settlers. Among Utah's famous are Robert Redford, born in California but now living in a Utah ski resort. Colorado was home to the late John Denver, the singer and songwriter known for songs such as *Windsong* and *Leaving on a Jet Plane*.

Which Wild West state first gave women the vote?

Wyoming is famous for its Wild West stories of cattle ranchers and wagon trains. Its pioneers were fur traders, who fought the Native Americans and took their territory. One of Wyoming's best known frontiersmen was Buffalo Bill Cody, who founded the town of Cody. Wyoming is named the Equality State, because in 1869 it was the first state to give women the full right to vote and to hold public office. The first woman governor in the United States was Nellie Taloe Ross, elected in Wyoming in 1925.

Which city is known as the "Mile High City"?

Denver, capital city of Colorado, calls itself the "Mile High City." It is the gateway to the Rocky Mountains, which dominate the western half of the state. Fifty-four of Colorado's mountains are above 14,000 ft (4,267 m) high.

What is the Devil's Tower?

Sixty million years ago, in northeastern Wyoming, molten lava forced its way up through sandstone rock and gradually cooled. Over the millennia, the sandstone was eroded until all that remained was the Devil's Tower—a fluted column of volcanic rock standing about 1,250 ft (381 m) high.

Old Faithful geyser, Yellowstone National Park

Which religious group founded Utah?

In 1847, Utah was Native American land. Then a religious group named the Mormons, persecuted in the East because the men of the sect took several wives, settled near Salt Lake and founded the state. Their leader, Brigham Young, became governor of the state. Even today, more than 70 percent of the people living in Utah are Mormons.

Where can you find a palace inside a cliff?

At Mesa Verde, Colorado, which has the best preserved cliff dwellings in America. The steep hill is riddled with more than 600 cave dwellings. One of these is known as the Cliff Palace, which has 217 rooms. Historians believe it was built about 1200.

Where is the largest living tree found?

San Francisco's Golden Gate Bridge was built in 1937.

In California. The General Sherman giant sequoia tree in Sequoia National Park is about 275 ft (85 m) high and weighs an estimated 2,500 tons.

Where is the lowest point in the western hemisphere?

Straddling the border between California and Nevada is Death Valley. It is a deep trough between two mountain ranges; 550 sq miles (1,424 sq km) of it lie 282 ft (86 m) below sea level. It is the lowest, and also the hottest, place in the western hemisphere.

The General Sherman is a giant sequoia tree.

What sort of chips can you find in Santa Clara?

In the 1970s and 1980s, a large number of electronics companies settled in the Santa Clara Valley, an area southwest of San Francisco, California. It later became known as Silicon Valley, after the material used to make computer chips.

Where can you visit a prison in a park?

At the Golden Gate National Park near San Francisco, California. The park includes shoreline, redwood forests, the National Maritime Museum, and the small island of Alcatraz. Alcatraz served as a maximum security prison from 1934 to 1963. Native Americans reclaimed it for a time in 1969.

Which state is the top of the pops?

Ever since California was admitted to the union in 1850, it has had the highest population of the U.S. To start with, it had a population of just under 10,000. By 1940, less than a century later, its population was 7 million! By 1970, California had more people than any other state in the U.S., and it has remained the most populated ever since. Los Angeles County alone has more citizens than at least 40 of the other states! Nowadays the population of California stands at just over 35 million.

What is Methuselah doing in Nevada?

Methuselah is the pet name of a giant bristlecone pine tree growing on Wheeler Peak, Nevada. It is thought to be the oldest living tree in America, at more than 4,600 years old.

What exploded at Frenchman's Flat and Yucca Flat?

Because Nevada has so few people, it has been used as a nuclear weapons test site. Frenchman's Flat and Yucca Flat, remote areas of southern Nevada, were used for exploding atomic bombs in 1951. In 1958, a ban on nuclear testing was declared, but in 1961 more nuclear weapons were exploded in Nevada, this time 3,800 ft (1,158 m) underground. Nuclear reactor research also began in Nevada, at the Las Vegas Bombing and Gunnery Range.

Which state has the grisliest criminal record in the U.S.?

California has the largest prison population of the U.S., with more than 160,000 inmates, the highest number of murders a year, and the most prisoners (both men and women) on death row (632 in 2003, 21 of whom were executed). Incidentally, the U.S. has the largest prison population in the world.

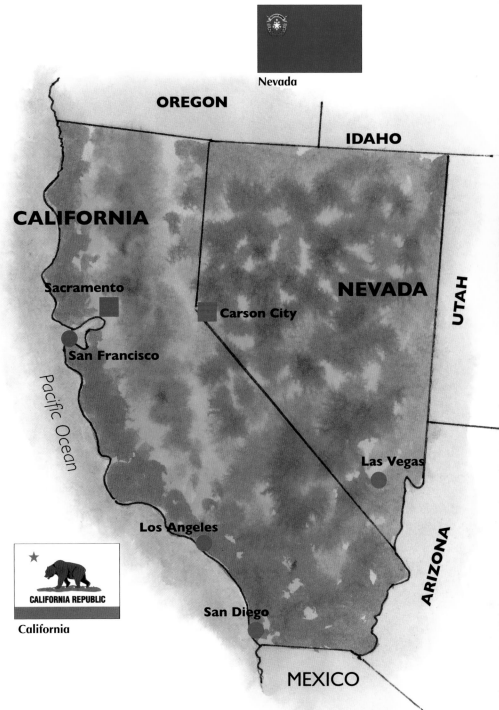

Nevada

CALIFORNIA REPUBLIC

California

Which state has the lowest rainfall?

Nevada has the lowest rainfall of any state of the union. Only about 9 in (23 cm) of rain falls every year in the northeast, while the area around Las Vegas receives less than 4 in (10 cm). The state is dominated by the Sierra Nevada mountain range, which rises along its western border and cuts off the damp winds that blow eastward from the Pacific Ocean.

Why do Texans remember the Alamo?

In 1836, during the war for independence from Mexico, the Alamo, a fort in San Antonio, was occupied by 189 Texas volunteers. It was besieged by thousands of Mexican troops and every American was killed. The Texan war cry from that day was: "Remember the Alamo!"

Where can you travel on the Devil's Road to see living organ pipes and Gila monsters?

One of Arizona's many strange habitats is the Organ Pipe Cactus National Monument, a park on the Mexican border. Here the rare organ pipe cactus grows to a height of 20 ft (6 m). The poisonous Gila monster, a type of lizard, also thrives here. A route across the Arizona desert was created in the 16th century by the expedition party of Melchoir Diaz, one of Coronado's captains. The route was named El Camino del Diablo, the Devil's Road. It was a punishing route; many of the pioneers who used it died on the way.

How many flags have flown over Texas?

Six! From 1519 to 1685 it was Spanish. In 1685 France claimed it for a short time, then about 1689 Spain retrieved it. Mexico was the next state to claim sovereignty, then from 1836 to 1845 it was independent. In 1845 it joined the United States—but from 1861 to 1865 it seceded to join the Confederacy!

What wildlife thrives in the desert?

Arizona, New Mexico, and Texas have rare desert plants. A hundred species of cacti thrive here. The agave and the yucca preserve water in their fleshy, waxy leaves. Animal life is varied too—there are coyotes, mountain lions, wildcats, and various deer, as well as scorpions, rattlesnakes, and many kinds of birds.

What massive sign of outer space can be seen near Winslow?

Near Winslow, Arizona, is a huge crater left by a massive asteroid that collided with the Earth long ago. The crater is 4,000 ft (1,220 m) wide and 600 ft (183 m) deep. Dust from the impact would have blocked out sunlight. The resulting climate change may be the reason why the dinosaurs died out, because they depended for their food on plants that could no longer grow.

How was William Bonney better known?

As Billy the Kid. He was born in New York, but moved to New Mexico as a child. He led a band of outlaws and claimed to have killed 27 men. Billy the Kid escaped from jail while awaiting execution and in 1881, aged 21 or 22, he was gunned down by the Sheriff Pat Garrett.

What is Sky City?

An ancient site of pueblo ruins and cliff dwellings in Cibola County, New Mexico. Multi-roomed houses were built into the caves in a sheer cliff that rises 337 ft (102 m) high. The dwellings have mud-walled rooms, and are still inhabited today by the Acoma people.

> The Alamo, in San Antonio, Texas. One of the Texans who tried to defend it was Davy Crocket.

What sent up a mushroom cloud at White Sands?

Los Alamos in New Mexico was one of America's first nuclear weapons research stations and the first atomic bomb in the world was assembled there. In 1945, the world's first nuclear weapon was detonated at White Sands, New Mexico.

White Sands, New Mexico

Arizona

UTAH

NEVADA

COLORADO

Santa Fe

Amarillo

ARIZONA

OKLAHOMA

CALIFORNIA

Phoenix

Albuquerque

Fort Worth

Dallas

Tucson

NEW MEXICO

Abilene

Texas

El Paso

TEXAS

MEXICO

Austin

Houston

San Antonio

Galveston

New Mexico

Where are the world's largest underground labyrinths?

Within the Guadalupe Mountains in Carlsbad Caverns National Park, New Mexico. The park contains 46,766 acres (20,000 hectares) of caves with stunning stalactites and stalagmites. About 30 miles (48 km) of labyrinth have so far been explored.

How did a computer develop from a radio shack?

The Tandy Corporation, based in Forth Worth, Texas, grew out of an electrical chain store named Radio Shack. In 1977, Tandy developed an affordable personal computer, the first computer to have a keyboard like the ones used today.

What did the Okies do?

The Okies were the Oklahoman farmers who were driven off their land by the great dust bowl—a combination of drought and winds that reduced the land to whirling dust where nothing would grow. The poverty-stricken families trekked across America to find work, but the economic depression made their task very difficult.

Many people in Oklahoma were forced by drought to pack up their homes and move on to find work.

How did Turkey Red transform the Great Plains?

The Great Plains are the potentially rich farming lands of Oklahoma, Kansas, and Nebraska. However, very dry summers there often meant that farmers lost all their crops to drought. When Mennonite settlers from Russia arrived in the Great Plains, they brought with them a special hardy type of wheat named Turkey Red. The Russian wheat was tough enough to survive the winter in the Great Plains, and if planted in the fall, was ready to harvest before the drought set in. By the early 1900s, Turkey Red was the main crop in the Great Plains.

Why might you recognize Scott's Bluff and Chimney Rock?

Because these famous landmarks on the old Oregon Trail have appeared in hundreds of Westerns. Chimney Rock is a sandstone pinnacle near the Platte River in Nebraska. Pioneer groups often camped beside it. Scott's Bluff in the west of Nebraska is an 800ft (244m) tall sand cliff beside the Platte River.

What is Arbor Day?

When the pioneers arrived in Nebraska, they discovered that there were very few trees. Arbor Day ("arbor" comes from the Latin for tree) was started by J. Sterling Morton, a journalist who later became the U.S. Secretary of Agriculture. On the very first Arbor Day, in 1872, over a million trees were planted—Nebraska's present-day forests owe their existence largely to this day.

Where are the Glass Mountains?

Near Fairview, Oklahoma, the mountains are covered in tiny selenite crystals, which from a distance make them sparkle like glass—hence the name. (There are also "Glass Mountains" in Texas.)

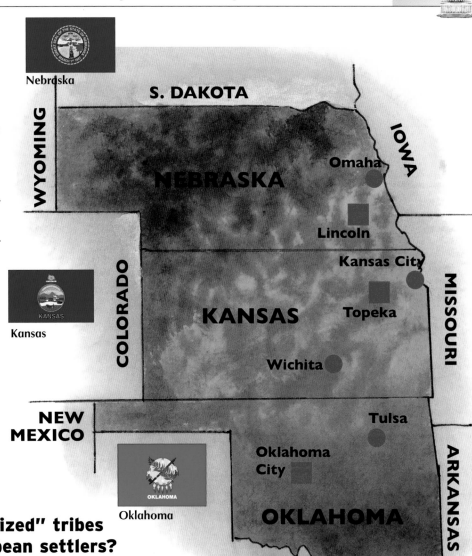

Nebraska

Kansas

Oklahoma

Why were the five "civilized" tribes cruelly treated by European settlers?

The Cherokees, Creeks, Choctaws, Chickasaws, and Seminoles were called "civilized" by European settlers because they allowed white people to take their lands, adopted white customs, and learned to read and write. In exchange for giving up their rich homelands to the whites, they were given a barren area—Oklahoma. They settled there and managed to survive. But when the whites saw the land could be lived on after all, they changed their minds. In 1889 they claimed most of Oklahoma too, pushing the "civilized" tribes into even smaller tracts of land.

Why is Oklahoma the Sooner state?

When the government decided to break its agreement with the Native Americans of Oklahoma and open up the land to white settlers, many settlers refused to wait for the official date to move there; to get their hands on the best land, they moved in sooner than was officially allowed. Hence the name.

Where can you see dinosaur footprints?

In the west of Oklahoma is an area known as the Panhandle region, a little strip of land that sticks out along the northern border of Texas. This area is rich in dinosaur fossils. In creek beds here, you can see dinosaur footprints made approximately 200 million years ago.

How much did Minuit pay for Manhattan?

When Peter Minuit arrived in America in 1626, Manhattan Island was occupied by the Wappinger Native Americans. He traded the island for some trinkets—worth about $24. The Wappinger thought they were selling the right to share the island, but the Dutch settler insisted it was a purchase.

Where did knickerbockers first get together?

At Hoboken, New Jersey, during the first ever organized game of baseball! The game received its official set of rules in 1845, when the Knickerbocker Baseball Club of New York City was founded. In 1846, the New York Base Ball Club defeated the New York Knickerbockers in their historic first game.

Who shed blood at Gettysburg?

In 1863, Gettysburg was the scene of the bloodiest battle of the American Civil War. Confederacy troops from the southern states invaded Union territory and threatened the crossroads town of Gettysburg in Pennsylvania. 31,000 Confederate men and 23,040 Union soldiers from the northern states were killed or wounded. The battle took three days, and though the Confederates came close to winning, in the end they lost both the battle and the war.

Manhattan is a center of broadcasting, publishing, and entertainment.

Who was America's first woman doctor?

When Elizabeth Blackwell decided to become a doctor, she could not get a school to accept her because she was a woman, and so she studied privately. Eventually the Geneva Medical School in western New York recognized her abilities and enrolled her. She graduated top of her class in 1849.

Which state is almost completely surrounded by water?

New Jersey! Well over 90 percent of its border is water. The Delaware River forms its western border, Delaware Bay and the Atlantic lie to the south, while its northeastern border follows the Hudson River.

Which east coast state has the most professional sports teams?

Pennsylvania has the most professional sports teams. They include the Philadelphia Phillies and Pittsburgh Pirates in baseball, the 76ers in basketball, the Pittsburgh Steelers and Philadelphia Eagles in football, and an ice hockey team—the Pittsburgh Penguins.

Pennyslvania

New Jersey

CANADA

VERMONT

Buffalo

Albany

MASS.

NEW YORK

L. Ontario

CONN.

L Erie

Scranton

Trenton

New York

PENNSYLVANIA

Atlantic Ocean

Harrisburg

OHIO

Philadelphia

NEW JERSEY

Pittsburg

MARYLAND

Dover

WEST VIRGINIA

WASHINGTON, D.C.

DELAWARE

New York

DECEMBER 7, 1787

Delaware

Where were America's first department stores?

Pennsylvania. John Wanamaker opened the first department store in 1876 in Philadelphia. Later, Frank Woolworth opened his first five-and-ten-cent stores in Utica, New York, and later in Lancaster, Pennsylvania. Other Pennsylvania chain stores were Kress and Grants.

What was the first capital of the United States?

New York. During the American Revolution, New York was one of the leading states. It was the 11th state to ratify the constitution. George Washington's inauguration ceremony took place in New York.

What is Massachusetts famous for?

Two main things! In 1620, at Cape Cod on the coast, the Pilgrims found a safe place to land and after their long voyage from England excitedly left the *Mayflower* and came ashore. Only 16 years later, Harvard University was founded in Cambridge. It is named after John Harvard, who left his books and half his estate to the college. Harvard has an impressive list of ex-students, including John F. Kennedy, e.e. cummings, Robert Frost, T.S. Eliot, Janet Reno, Mary Robinson, and actor Tommy Lee Jones.

Which state relies on lobsters and chickens?

Maine is famous for its delicious lobsters, which are pulled out of the waters of the Atlantic Ocean. Also famous are Maine's broiler chickens, which are reared there and then exported all over the country.

Which teacher dreamed of going into space?

A social studies teacher in Concord, New Hampshire, who in 1985 applied to become a member of the space shuttle team. Tragically, the *Challenger* shuttle exploded over the Atlantic Ocean a few seconds after take-off, killing everyone on board.

Present-day Cape Cod, Massachusetts, where the Pilgrims landed in 1620

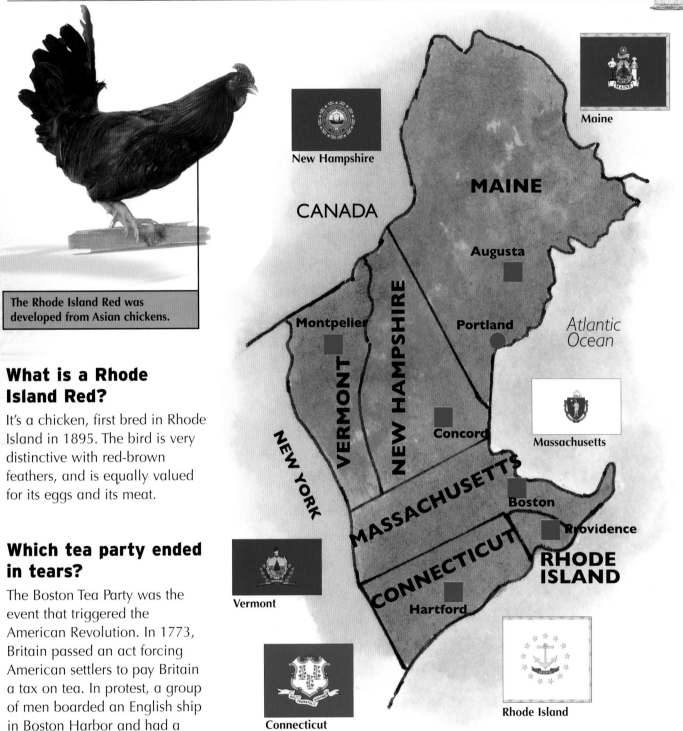

The Rhode Island Red was developed from Asian chickens.

What is a Rhode Island Red?

It's a chicken, first bred in Rhode Island in 1895. The bird is very distinctive with red-brown feathers, and is equally valued for its eggs and its meat.

Which tea party ended in tears?

The Boston Tea Party was the event that triggered the American Revolution. In 1773, Britain passed an act forcing American settlers to pay Britain a tax on tea. In protest, a group of men boarded an English ship in Boston Harbor and had a "tea party," throwing the cargo of tea overboard. The British government responded with punishments against the state and shortly afterwards war broke out between the British and the settlers.

Where is America's oldest synagogue?

In Newport, Rhode Island. The Touro Synagogue was built between 1759 and 1763. From its earliest days Rhode Island was known for its tolerance of all religious faiths. The Touro Synagogue is now a national monument.

Who took to the air at Kill Devil Hill?

The first powered manned flight in the world took place on December 17, 1903, at Kill Devil Hill near Kitty Hawk in North Carolina. The aircraft was built by Wilbur Wright (1867–1912) and his brother Orville (1871–1948) and had a four-cylinder gasoline engine (which they built themselves), a propeller, and two parallel sets of wings. Orville Wright flew the plane while his brother Wilbur lay alongside the engine on the lower wing. The plane flew for just 12 seconds and covered a distance of 120 ft (36 m).

What was the dreadful Trail of Tears?

The Cherokee lived peacefully in South Carolina, where they had established farms and schools and developed their own written language. But the whites could not tolerate living with them and in 1838 forced them out. They drove them west, along what became known as the Trail of Tears, because so many of them died.

How did John Brown die for human rights?

John Brown was a leader in the fight against slavery. In 1859, he led an attack on a federal arsenal (weapons store) at Harper's Ferry, Virginia (now West Virginia). He wanted the weapons to liberate slaves. His men took some soldiers hostage. The local militia were sent against them and Brown's men surrendered. Brown was tried and hanged for inciting rebellion, treason, and murder.

Which state heard the first gunshots of the Civil War?

On December 20, 1860, South Carolina became the first state to secede from the Union. Ten others followed. The first shots of the Civil War were fired in South Carolina by Confederate troops.

Baltimore is the largest city in Maryland. It is an important shipbuilding center.

The Wrights' airplane was built in a bicycle factory.

Maryland

West Virginia

Where did the British first settle in America?

The Virginia Company of London sent out three ships to establish a colony in America and find something profitable to send back to England. In 1607 the sailors established Jamestown on Chesapeake Bay, Virginia. After three years of hardship they were ready to return home, but the colony was saved when its new governor, Lord De La Warr, arrived from England with supplies. In 1612 the settlers began tobacco farming, and from that time the colony thrived.

Where can a wild turkey find refuge?

Wild turkeys used to flourish in South Carolina, but over the years they were hunted almost to extinction. Now there is a turkey refuge in South Carolina in the Francis Marion National Forest. Here turkeys are bred and released into the wild.

PENNSYLVANIA

OHIO

MARYLAND

Baltimore

Annapolis

WEST VIRGINIA

WASHINGTON, D.C.

Charleston

Richmond

Norfolk

KENTUCKY

VIRGINIA

Raleigh

TENNESSEE

NORTH CAROLINA

Columbia

Atlantic Ocean

Virginia

SOUTH CAROLINA

GEORGIA

Charleston

South Carolina

North Carolina

Whose home was in Memphis?

Born in Tupelo, Mississippi, Elvis Presley moved to Memphis, Tennessee, as a teenager. When he became a superstar he bought Graceland, a mansion just outside the town. He lived there with his wife, and later during the years that he spent alone before he died. It was at Graceland that he died of heart failure in 1977. The mansion is now a site of pilgrimage for his millions of fans. Elvis was the highest-paid performer in the history of show business.

The Gateway Arch in St. Louis, Missouri, is a memorial to the pioneers of the West.

What was the "monkey trial"?

In the early 1900s, biologist Charles Darwin claimed that people were descended from apes. This upset many Christians, who believed that Adam and Eve were our first ancestors. The Church was strong in the state of Tennessee, and a law was passed there making it illegal to teach Darwin's theories in schools. But in the early 1920s, John Scopes, a biology teacher in Dayton, Tennessee, began to teach Darwin's theory. In 1925 he was charged with breaking the law and fined $100 in a famous trial that became known as the "monkey trial."

Why are Fulbright students always on the move?

The Fulbright scholarship is an exchange program that helps American students to study abroad and students from overseas to study in America. It is open to graduates, and was started by Senator J. William Fulbright of Arkansas in 1946.

Where can you visit a diamond mine?

The only state in the U.S. to have produced diamonds is Arkansas, which has a diamond on its flag. Diamonds were first discovered there in 1906. Today the Crater of Diamonds State Park is open to the public.

Where was the most violent earthquake ever recorded in the U.S.?

At New Madrid, Missouri, in the winter of 1811–1812. The quake registered from Canada to the Gulf of Mexico, and there were at least 1,874 aftershocks. It is thought it would have measured 8.4 on the Richter scale, but fortunately very few people died.

When can a horse win a crown in Kentucky?

The most important and popular event of the year in Kentucky is the Kentucky Derby, which is part of the Triple Crown in the horse-racing calendar. The first Derby was run in 1875 at Churchill Downs in Louisville, Kentucky.

Elvis Presley was probably the most famous entertainer of the 20th century.

Who named Kentucky paradise?

Daniel Boone was a famous pioneer and hunter in the early days of American settlement. He loved the Kentucky countryside, where he saw herds of buffalo roaming across the plains, vast tracts of forest alive with deer and wild turkeys, and rivers full of fish. To him Kentucky was a hunter's paradise.

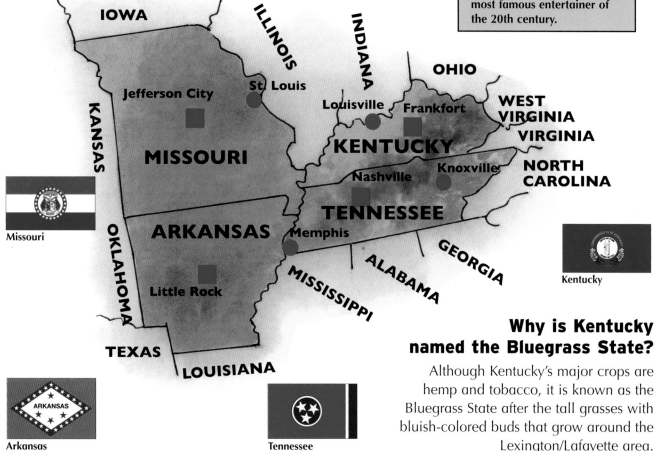

Missouri

Arkansas

Tennessee

Kentucky

Why is Kentucky named the Bluegrass State?

Although Kentucky's major crops are hemp and tobacco, it is known as the Bluegrass State after the tall grasses with bluish-colored buds that grow around the Lexington/Lafayette area.

Which U.S. citizens were first to shoot into space?

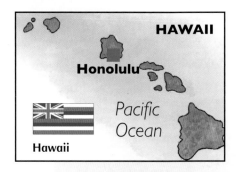

HAWAII

Honolulu

Pacific Ocean

Hawaii

In 1961, Alan Shepard took off from Cape Canaveral in Florida—America's major launch site for most of its space exploration projects. This was the first manned American flight. It was suborbital and lasted 15 minutes. The following year, John Glenn became the first American to orbit the Earth. His flight lasted just 4 hours and 55 minutes.

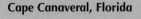
Cape Canaveral, Florida

What happened to Captain Cook when he reached Hawaii?

In 1778, Captain Cook arrived in Hawaii and named the islands the Sandwich Islands after his sponsor, the Earl of Sandwich. He got on well with the islanders until 1779, when they quarreled over the theft of one of the Captain's boats. Going ashore to recover his boat from the Native Indian thieves, Cook was ambushed in a fight and killed.

What was the worst natural disaster in recent U.S. history?

In 1992, Hurricane Andrew hit the coast of Florida and devastated Florida City and a town named Homestead. It then went on to the Gulf Coast states, where Morgan City and Lafayette in Louisiana suffered terrible damage. In all, Hurricane Andrew caused $27 billion worth of damage and left an estimated 58 dead.

Where do trees have their roots in the air?

In the Everglades National Park in Florida, a vast saltwater swamp full of mangrove trees. It was named "Everglades" because it seems like an endless expanse of green glades. Mangrove trees thrive in tidal salt water. When the tide goes out, their roots are exposed to the air. Alligators bask in the swamp, and the trees are home to many kinds of birds including spoonbills, brown pelicans, ospreys, and bald eagles.

Alabama

Georgia

Florida

Louisiana

Mississippi

Who wrote about a mockingbird?

Harper Lee. Born in Monroeville, Alabama, she studied law, but got a job as an airline ticket clerk before quitting it to become a writer. Her novel *To Kill A Mockingbird* won the Pulitzer Prize in 1961 and was made into a movie starring Gregory Peck. It is about the trial of an innocent black man.

> The Mississippi River was used as a major transportation route by Union forces in the Civil War.

Where did people live in a cave for 8,000 years?

At the Russell Caves near Bridgeport, Alabama. The caves extend miles into the mountainside, and the one closest to the entrance shows signs that humans must have lived there for over 8,000 years. The caves were declared a national monument in 1961.

Who erected a monument to a boll weevil?

The boll weevil is a bug that eats the heart of the cotton seed, destroying the crop. Many southern states grew nothing but cotton until 1915, when a plague of boll weevils ate everything and forced them to grow different things. Although 1915 was a disaster for the farmers, when they grew more crops in following years, they were better off. So in gratitude, the farmers of Enterprise, Alabama, erected a monument to the boll weevil.

What terrible air disaster happened in Chicago?

In 1979, an engine fell off a DC-10 as it was taking off from O' Hare Airport, Chicago. The plane flew out of control and crashed. All 271 people on board were killed, as well as two people on the ground.

Which brothers from Dayton, Ohio, pioneered air travel?

The Wright brothers made their first powered flight in North Carolina, but they lived and designed their planes in Dayton, Ohio. The brothers lived together all their lives and enjoyed mechanics from a very young age. They opened a bicycle repair shop and also made their own bicycles. It was a short leap from bicycles to gliders. They built their first glider in 1900 and went on to construct the first manned powered airplane.

What made Sarah Breedlove rich?

Born in 1867 in Louisiana, Sarah Breedlove invented a formula for straightening curly hair. She began by selling her product from door to door in 1905. Her business grew and she opened the Madam C. Walker Manufacturing Company in Indianapolis. Sarah Breedlove was the first black American woman in the U.S. to become a millionaire.

Why was Anthony Wayne called "mad"?

"Mad" Anthony Wayne was an early pioneer who got his nickname when he stormed a British fort in a surprise night attack. He fought Native Americans in the Battle of Fallen Timbers, and helped drive them out of Ohio, Indiana, Michigan, Illinois, and Wisconsin.

How did Toni win world recognition?

Toni Morrison grew up in Lorain, Ohio, and attended Howard and Cornell Universities. Her novel *Beloved* won the 1987 Pulitzer Prize and in 1993 she was the first black woman to win the Nobel Prize for Literature.

Chicago is famous for its architecture. One of the world's first skyscrapers was built in Chicago in 1885.

Who was America's first woman doctor?

When Elizabeth Blackwell decided to become a doctor, she could not get a school to accept her because she was a woman, and so she studied privately. Eventually the Geneva Medical School in western New York recognized her abilities and enrolled her. She graduated top of her class in 1849.

Which state is almost completely surrounded by water?

New Jersey! Well over 90 percent of its border is water. The Delaware River forms its western border, Delaware Bay and the Atlantic lie to the south, while its northeastern border follows the Hudson River.

Pennyslvania

New Jersey

New York

Delaware

DECEMBER 7, 1787

Which east coast state has the most professional sports teams?

Pennsylvania has the most professional sports teams. They include the Philadelphia Phillies and Pittsburgh Pirates in baseball, the 76ers in basketball, the Pittsburgh Steelers and Philadelphia Eagles in football, and an ice hockey team—the Pittsburgh Penguins.

Where were America's first department stores?

Pennsylvania. John Wanamaker opened the first department store in 1876 in Philadelphia. Later, Frank Woolworth opened his first five-and-ten-cent stores in Utica, New York, and later in Lancaster, Pennsylvania. Other Pennsylvania chain stores were Kress and Grants.

What was the first capital of the United States?

New York. During the American Revolution, New York was one of the leading states. It was the 11th state to ratify the constitution. George Washington's inauguration ceremony took place in New York.

What is Massachusetts famous for?

Two main things! In 1620, at Cape Cod on the coast, the Pilgrims found a safe place to land and after their long voyage from England excitedly left the *Mayflower* and came ashore. Only 16 years later, Harvard University was founded in Cambridge. It is named after John Harvard, who left his books and half his estate to the college. Harvard has an impressive list of ex-students, including John F. Kennedy, e.e. cummings, Robert Frost, T.S. Eliot, Janet Reno, Mary Robinson, and actor Tommy Lee Jones.

Which state relies on lobsters and chickens?

Maine is famous for its delicious lobsters, which are pulled out of the waters of the Atlantic Ocean. Also famous are Maine's broiler chickens, which are reared there and then exported all over the country.

Which teacher dreamed of going into space?

A social studies teacher in Concord, New Hampshire, who in 1985 applied to become a member of the space shuttle team. Tragically, the *Challenger* shuttle exploded over the Atlantic Ocean a few seconds after take-off, killing everyone on board.

Present-day Cape Cod, Massachusetts, where the Pilgrims landed in 1620

Michigan

ILLINOIS

Illinois

Indiana

Ohio

Who was the first woman to run for presidency?

Victoria Claflin Woodhull (1838–1927) was born in Homer, Ohio. She was an activist and social reformer, and the first woman to be nominated as a presidential candidate. She stood for the presidency in 1872 as a representative of the Equal Rights Party, but was not elected. Later in life she also supported the idea of eugenics—which means allowing only beautiful and intelligent people to have children.

Where is America's largest prison?

Mississippi. Its State Penitentiary is the largest in the U.S. with more than 1,500 inmates. Ohio has the second largest Federal Correctional Institute in the U.S. with more than 47,200 people.

What caused the states of Ohio and Michigan to nearly go to war?

Ohio and Michigan both claimed they owned an area around Toledo. In 1836, the two states called out their armies and were ready to fight. Then Congress gave the area to Ohio, and gave Michigan some land in the Upper Peninsula. Both states were satisfied with this.

Who is Steveland Judkins Morris?

He is better known as Stevie Wonder. He was born blind in Saginaw, Michigan, in 1950. During the 1970s and 1980s, he recorded many smash hits on the Tamla Motown record label.

One of Stevie Wonder's biggest hits was "Superstition".

Native Americans

Who first discovered America?

Many thousands of years before Christopher Columbus sailed across the Atlantic from Europe, people trekked into North America across a land bridge from Siberia. This is thought to have happened about 13,000 or more years ago, when the last Ice Age was coming to an end. Some historians believe that people may also have been living in America long before this, and that some of them may have moved north into southwestern North America.

Cornplanter, an Iroquois chief

What started at 4 a.m. in 1607?

The first permanent English settlement in the U.S. One settler said: "About foure in the morning, wee descried the Land of Virginia." The settler went on to say, "...[we] got good store of Mussels and Oysters, which lay upon the ground as thicke as stones."

Who left behind only their burial mounds?

The Hopewell people, who lived in the valleys of Ohio and Illinois for 1,500 years from 300 B.C.E. The little that is known about their culture comes from objects found in their burial mounds. These mounds were as much as 200 ft (61 m) in circumference.

Pottery, stone ornaments, and clay images have been excavated from Hopewell burial mounds.

Who had a good government before the Europeans?

Five tribes, former enemies, came together and formed the Iroquois Confederacy possibly in the late 15th century Decisions were made by a council of men, who were elected for life. Women had the right to dismiss any of them.

Who was inspired by the Iroquois government?

Benjamin Franklin, co-author of the Constitution. He thought the idea of a government like the Iroquois Confederacy could be used by the English colonies. The eagle on the United States' shield is the Iroquois bald eagle, also a symbol for the Iroquois nation.

Where did Native Americans get their horses?

For a long time, it was thought there were no horses in North America until the Spanish brought them in 1519. But fossil records show evidence of horses there long before this. At some unknown date they disappeared, only to be reintroduced by the Spanish.

Which people were given a name meaning "those who have vanished"?

The Hohokam people, who lived near Mexico in the Arizona desert over 2,000 years ago. They survived by irrigating their crops using canals. They were given their name by the Pima people, who later came to the region where "those who have vanished" once lived.

How many Native Americans lived in America before Europeans arrived?

Impossible to know for sure. Some historians estimate that it was less than 1.5 million. Others say these numbers are far too low for such a vast land. They give figures of between 8 and 18 million.

Why were Native Americans called "Indians"?

Before America was known to Europeans, the explorer Christopher Columbus planned to sail westward around the world to reach India. After a journey lasting more than two months, he finally reached land—probably the Bahamas—and, thinking he had arrived in India, called the people there Indians! The name stuck and became a label for all the different Native Americans living in the New World.

Columbus meets non-Europeans in the New World.

Who did the settlers call "civilized"?

The Choctaw, Cherokee, Creek, Chicksaw, and Seminole tribes, living in the southeast of North America, were called the "Five Civilized Tribes" by early white settlers. They were given this name because of similarities between their cultures and those of the Europeans. The tribes lived in planned villages, were farmers as well as hunters, and some were wealthy enough to own slaves. Later, some of them became Christians and adopted other aspects of the settlers' lives.

Osceola was the leader of the Seminole people, who lived in present-day Florida and Georgia.

Which Native Americans believed seven was a sacred number?

The Cherokee. They held seven ceremonies, six of which took place each year and the seventh every seven years. Their seven clans were based in seven "mother towns."

A Mandan village by the bank of the Missouri River

What is special about the Seminole people of Florida?

They are a mixed group, formed from the survivors of various Florida tribes—mostly Creek Indians—after the European slave trade had almost wiped them out. The Creek were joined by runaway black slaves, and successfully resisted attempts to root them out from the swamps.

Was there really a Sioux tribe?

No. The word Sioux was adopted by French explorers who picked it up from the Chippewa tribe. Sioux is a Chippewa word for "snake," or "enemies to the west." The Chippewa used it to describe the Lakota people, whom they had pushed westward from the Western Great Lakes. So the Sioux are really the Lakota, a name that means "where the people of peace dwell," or "friends."

Which people hunted and farmed by the Missouri River in North Dakota?

The Mandans hunted buffalo, like other Plains people, but they also lived in permanent villages built high up on the banks of the Missouri River. They farmed the land and grew corn. The explorers Lewis and Clark spent a winter with the Mandans before heading west.

Which Native Americans worked together as one large family?

The Creek people divided their land into family plots, which were farmed by everybody working together as equals, including their chief. Some of the harvest was set aside and stored in a special building, to be shared by everyone on public occasions.

Where did the Apache come from?

They came from northwestern Canada, where they had lived as hunters and where farming was impossible. Their migration to the southwest began about C.E. 850 and continued until about 1500.

Which native people helped two white Americans explore west of the Mississippi?

The Nez Perce people helped the two explorers, Lewis and Clark, in their travels across what was to the white men an unknown land. They built canoes for them and drew maps of the rivers, which enabled the explorers eventually to reach the Pacific Ocean.

What is a hogan?

The Navajo people of the southwest lived in beehive-shaped houses called hogans. A hogan was made from a framework of pinewood poles, or sometimes stone, covered with dried mud. The Navajo still like to have hogans on their land, close to their modern houses.

What was dried buffalo dung used for?

It made a useful fuel for cooking and for keeping warm, because when it burned it was almost smokeless. The little smoke produced by the fire escaped through a gap at the top of the tepee created by a flap in the buffalo hide.

The inside of a tepee was warm and comfortable.

Who welcomed the morning Sun from the rooftops?

The Mandans, who lived in domed timber lodges covered with layers of grass and sods of earth. Such a sturdy structure could easily support the weight of the village elders, who climbed onto the rooftops at dawn to greet the Sun each day.

What are sweat lodges?

Plains peoples used these for religious ceremonies. They were windowless and dome-shaped. Inside the lodge, water was poured over large, hot stones to generate heat and steam.

The apartments of the Pueblo peoples

Did the Native Americans have toothbrushes and hairbrushes?

Of course! Porcupine hairs were used for bristles and sometimes a stick was cut into the right shape and frayed at the edges to make a toothbrush. The tail of a porcupine was used to make a hairbrush.

Who lived in thatched houses?

The Choctaw people, who lived in the semitropical southeast. They used the leaves of the palmetto, a small palm tree, as thatch for their houses. This allowed the air to circulate better than a wood, stone, or brick roof, and prevented their houses from becoming uncomfortably hot inside.

Who lived in longhouses?

Iroquois tribes lived in groups of up to 100 people in long, narrow houses about 25 ft (7.6 m) wide and 150–220 ft (45–67 m) long. The houses were built from wooden poles covered with strips of tree bark. Inside, platforms against the walls were used as beds and benches, and the earthen floors were covered with more bark or woven mats. Partitions divided one family area from another, but "neighbors" sometimes shared a cooking fire.

Who were the first Americans to live in "apartments"?

Some 1,500 years ago, the Anasazi built homes like apartment blocks out of adobe (sun-dried mud bricks). They were located in canyons and at the entrances to caves in Arizona and New Mexico. The ruins of one site, Pueblo Bonito, show that it was home to over 1,000 people. In the 1500s, the Pueblos also built rows of adobe houses up to five stories high. They reached the upper stories by climbing connecting ladders.

Who hunted in disguise?

The Cherokee, Creek, and Choctaw hunted deer instead of buffalo, as there were no buffalo on their land. A solitary deer was tracked by a lone hunter, who sometimes wore a deer's hide as camouflage, and imitated a deer's mating call to attract his prey.

What are the three sisters?

Corn, beans, and squash were called the three sisters by the Iroquois. They were so important as sources of food that they were thought of as female spirits. Corn was a valuable source of carbohydrate; beans were a source of protein; and squash provided important vitamins. European settlers learned from Native Americans how to grow pumpkins, and made them into one of their traditional foods for Thanksgiving: sweet pumpkin pie.

What can you find to eat in a desert?

More than you might think. Most cacti have edible fruit. Some cacti fruit need cooking, but prickly pears can be eaten raw once their thorns have been removed. Some cacti have seeds that can be pounded to make flour, and some have edible roots.

What did the Navajo learn from the Spanish?

Originally the Navajo were nomadic hunters. They learned about farming crops and sheep from the Pueblo Indians and later the Spanish, who arrived in the 1500s. The Navajo stole sheep from the Spanish, and in time became expert sheep farmers.

A Cherokee hunter approaches his prey downwind of them.

Who ate fast food?

The Shoshone, the Paiute, and other peoples who lived in the Great Basin, a land so arid that it could not be farmed. They never stayed in the same place for long, but moved around, living off food that they gathered or dug up—for example, grasshoppers, lizards, roots, berries, seeds, and nuts. They were very close to their environment, but Europeans did not understand this and called them "Digger Indians."

What was pemmican?

Pemmican was buffalo meat pounded and mixed with berries and fat to produce a type of dried food. It was stored and used later when fresh food was hard to find. Pemmican was high in protein and could be stored for years if necessary.

How was food boiled without pans?

Simple. A hole was dug, lined with rawhide to prevent leaking, and filled with water into which red-hot stones were dropped. The stones made the water hot enough to boil meat, and more stones from the fire could be added as necessary.

Who has boomerangs that do not come back?

The Hopi people use a curved stick, about the same size as a boomerang, to throw through the air and bring down rabbits. Hopi hunters gather in a large circle, up to a mile wide, and move forward together. When a rabbit appears, a nearby hunter throws his rabbit stick.

How was antelope meat preserved?

Native peoples dried the meat of deer, antelope, turkey, and rabbit in the sun. They then added salt as a preservative. Salt was collected from salt springs by boiling away the water, or by scraping it from a salt bed.

Spearing fish required patience and skill.

Who did not bury the dead?

Some of the Plains peoples placed the bodies of their dead on a scaffold or in trees to keep them safe from wild animals while they decayed. The Huron people placed the bodies of their dead in coffins, which were kept above ground on poles for up to 15 years before the bones were buried.

Did native peoples trade with one another?

Yes, at fixed times of the year they came together at special meeting places to trade. Nomadic peoples from the Plains with surplus buffalo skins traded them for farm produce from settled tribes.

Who hunted for heavyweight prey?

The Plains people lived by hunting the mighty buffalo, a hefty creature at about 6 ft (2 m) high and 1 ton (1,000 kg) in weight. Despite its great weight, it could run very fast. Before horses were used, Plains hunters disguised in animal skins sneaked up on the buffalo. Sometimes they would stampede them over cliffs or into pens. On horseback, a buffalo was brought down with spears, and bows and arrows tipped with iron or stone. Bows were specially strengthened and shortened to under 3 ft (1 m), for easier use on horseback.

How valuable were eagle feathers?

Around 1850, a valuable horse could be exchanged for 15 eagle feathers. The value of the feathers came from their scarcity and religious importance. Especially valuable were the more colorful feathers of young eagles that took a long time to capture. Prized feathers were used to decorate headdresses and costumes.

How did Native Americans record their history?

They painted a record of past events in picture-writing and symbols on animal hides. They also passed on the tribe's history by word-of-mouth to the next generation.

Where do moccasins come from?

"Moccasin" is an Algonquian word for a type of footwear made from buffalo or deer hides. The soles were made from hard, untanned skin (rawhide), and the uppers from soft, tanned skin. The two parts were sewed together with thread made from rawhide or the sinews of the animal, and the uppers decorated with beads or colored feather quills. Moccasins were made by women, and different tribes had their own designs.

Were feathers worn just for fun?

Moccasins came in many different styles. Apaches even wore long ones up to the knee.

No. Feathers were worn by some peoples for decorative or ritual purposes. Among the Lakota (Sioux) people, only a warrior who had proved his courage in battle was allowed to wear the elaborate eagle-feather headdress that reached from head to toe. Eagle feathers were highly prized, because they were thought to possess spiritual power.

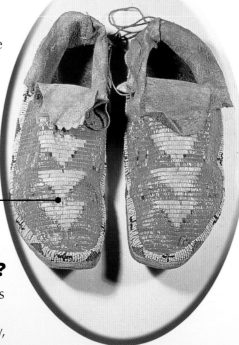

On which part of the body was a roach worn?

On the head—because a roach is a headdress made from dyed animal hair attached to a narrow, flat piece of bone that fits onto the head. The most important kind of roach was decorated with one or more feathers to show victory or bravery in battle.

How did the Pima and Papago keep warm in the winter?

The Pima and Papago came from the southwest and wore few clothes in the hot climate. When the temperature dropped in the winter, they kept themselves warm by rubbing animal grease onto their bare upper bodies for insulation.

Possessions, like this warrior's headdress and feathers, were left close to the corpse.

Why was a bear claw necklace highly prized?

The killing of a bear was an extremely dangerous activity, and it happened so rarely that the claws were very valuable. A bear claw necklace was a highly prized piece of jewelry.

Who walked on yucca?

The Paiute lived in an extremely dry, semidesert environment, where there were no buffalo to provide leather for moccasins. However, the fiber of the yucca, a desert plant, could be woven into moccasins that were light and comfortable for the climate.

How did Plains men celebrate their first kill?

When a young man killed his first buffalo, he was offered the tastiest part of the tongue as a reward—but he was expected to share it among his friends as a sign of his generosity rather than eat it himself. In fact, to show his maturity, he would decline to eat any of the first animal he killed.

Which peoples trace their descent through their mothers?

Lots of native peoples, including the Iroquois, Cherokee, Choctaw, Creek, Apalachee, Navajo, and Apache, trace their descent through the mother's side of their families. When an Apache male married, he always went to live in the home of his wife's mother.

A buffalo hunt was dangerous, but the rewards were great.

Who stopped eating clumsy turtles?

Many Native American peoples had rituals for their children before they were even born. People like the Nez Perce and the Northern Shoshone had ritual prayers for men who wanted to be fathers. Pregnant mothers had their own prayers, and followed a special diet, giving up meat and eating only fish and birds. A pregnant Iroquois woman stopped eating turtles in the hope that her baby would not grow up clumsy on land, like a turtle. In Navajo communities, pregnant women untied their braided hair, and freed animals like horses, hoping to create a free passage and safe birth for the baby.

Papooses were safe and sturdy, and nicer to look at than modern ones!

How did babies travel with their parents?

In a papoose (originally an Algonquian word). The papoose was made of soft animal skin and had a stiff backboard woven from twigs. It was tied onto the mother's back and the baby was held in a comfortable upright position, able to see its surroundings. Some papooses had sharp, projecting wooden points on the outsides, so if they fell off while the mother was riding, the points would stick into the ground and protect the baby. Heavy padding at the top of the papoose formed a sun shield.

How did Pueblo men prove their manhood?

Pueblo peoples organized mock battles between the young men and older men in their communities. In order to be accepted as an adult, a young man had to show his courage and strength without injuring anyone.

Who had to kill to become a man?

People like the Chicksaw, Creek, and Choctaw expected a young man to become a man by wounding or killing an enemy in battle. Only after he had done this was the man granted an adult name, and a celebration was held to honor the event.

What happened before a marriage took place?

A marriage among Plains peoples depended on the man being able to offer some horses as a dowry to his future father-in-law. An Iroquois man would give a present to his future wife instead; they usually had a trial marriage before they agreed to the real thing.

How was a trial marriage organized?

Among the Hopi people, a "dumaiya" was a kind of trial marriage: the woman lived with her boyfriend's family for a few days. If the family were happy with the arrangement, a formal wedding ceremony was held.

How did Navajo girls celebrate growing up?

The first laugh of a child, and reaching the age of seven, were both marked with festivities. When a girl reached puberty, there was a ceremony called the Kinalda (still held today), in which she was covered in mud.

What does a shaman do?

A shaman, sometimes mistakenly called a witch-doctor, is a man or woman who is able to talk to the spirits and persuade them to do things. Shamans are especially valued for their ability to heal the sick by driving out harmful spirits from the body. They practice herbal medicine, and often work themselves into a trancelike state, experiencing spiritual visions.

White Buffalo was a shaman of the Blackfeet tribe.

What are thunder pipes?

Plains peoples felt that thunder and lightning were punishments sent down on them by the spirits. They needed to be on good terms with the spirits to avoid their anger, so they gathered together for the ritual smoking of thunder pipes—colorful pipes decorated with eagle feathers and bells.

Why are eagles sacred?

Many native peoples thought of eagles as messengers between the spirit world and humans. They created special dances to imitate the eagle's flight.

Who wore masks?

Ritual ceremonies were held by many native peoples as a way of getting in touch with the spirit world. Masks played an important role. They were designed and painted in special ways to show the spirits' natures, and to help attract supernatural beings.

What were False Faces?

False Faces were the sacred masks worn by the Iroquois shamans. The masks were thought to attract helpful spirits that would scare away spirits that caused diseases and trouble. The fierce-looking masks were worn in rituals to restore health to the sick.

Why is the Great Turtle important to the Iroquois?

The Great Turtle is the supreme animal in the Iroquois creation story. When the world was made of only water, the turtle caught a pregnant woman who fell from the sky. It dived into the deep, returned with bits of earth that fell with the woman, and helped create the world.

Where is the spirit world?

Everywhere! The world of the Native Americans is filled every which way with spiritual forces. The spirits are seen mostly as kindly, but sometimes as capable of doing harm to the human world. They live in nature, and nearly everything—from a glorious eagle to a humble seed of corn—is believed to have spiritual powers. Aspects of life such as illness or climate are still understood by Native Americans to be ruled by the spirits.

Who did the spirits command to walk backward?

Special warriors among the Lakota people were directed by spirits to lead their lives backward. They would only walk forward when they meant to go backward, and use "yes" and "no" in their opposite senses. But in battle they behaved like ordinary warriors!

A shaman is part doctor, psychiatrist, prophet, and ghost-hunter.

Who made spirit dolls?

Pueblo peoples such as the Hopi believed that the Kachina spirits helped to bring rain and renew the land ready for the next growing season. The Hopi gave Kachina dolls to their children to teach them about the different types of spirits.

What are totem poles?

Totem poles are carved and decorated wooden poles that Native Americans of the northwest, such as the Haida, erected outside their homes to advertise their family's status. Some poles were more than 40 ft (12 m) tall; they were usually carved in the shape of animals or birds that held a special meaning for the family clan and its ancestors. Each family had its own symbols and designs. Totem poles were also erected as a memorial to a deceased ancestor.

Who was kidnapped for blankets?

The Navajo began weaving blankets for their own use. Their work was so artistic that settlers in New Mexico kidnapped them and forced them to weave blankets for them. Some of these "slave blankets" are now world-famous works of art.

What do Native Americans use to make music?

Music is an essential part of religious, social, and military life. Logs were hollowed out to form drums of all sizes and the tops covered with tightly stretched animal skins. Turtle shells were turned into rattles, and hollowed bones made pipes that were blown in battle.

What are sandpaintings?

Trains of colored sand are painstakingly positioned to form a complicated design of geometric shapes and symbols. Sandpaintings are a way of recording events using symbols. Today, sandpaintings are kept as works of art, but traditionally they were wiped away when a religious ritual was over.

Sandpaintings have been part of Navajo rituals for many generations.

Christians mistakenly thought that totem poles were statues to gods.

Who were the greatest tattooists?

Without a doubt, they were the Timucua people of Florida. The Timucua wore little clothing because of the hot climate. They liked to decorate most of their bodies with amazingly complicated patterns. Both men and women wore the tattoos. The Mojave people of northern California specialized in facial tattooing to show their family status, while Osage women liked tattooing spiders on the backs of their hands. People on the northwest coast used tattooing to record their family's history.

Who is a famous Tlingit?

Larry McNeil is a Tlingit from Alaska, famous for his photography and his work as a professor at the Institute of American Indian Arts in Santa Fé. He became a photographer after realizing that Alaskan Native Americans were not fairly represented in art.

Who had beautiful battle shields?

The Crow people were famous for the care and artistry they put into their battle shields. The shields were about 1–2 ft (30–61 cm) in diameter, made of rawhide, and painted with symbols that had a personal meaning to their creator.

What do we know about the Hopewell?

The Hopewell people, who once lived in the southeastern United States, have been extinct for 500 years. Little is known about their culture. But their large burial mounds have been excavated to reveal paintings that tell the stories of complicated funeral ceremonies and rituals.

Who were, and still are, master potters?

Pueblo peoples such as the Zuni and Hopi are the master potters of the Native American world. Centuries of experience have been passed down to today's generation of potters, who turn out beautifully crafted and finely painted ceramics.

Who made beautiful blue jewelry?

The Navajo became expert artistic jewelers in the 1870s. They produce fine necklaces and belts decorated with turquoise, a beautiful blue-green precious stone.

Why is the Little Bighorn famous?

The U.S. Army was defeated by a combined force of Lakota (Sioux), Cheyenne, and Arapaho warriors. The Native Americans were resisting government demands to move to reservations. The army planned to block off possible escape routes and divided its regiment into groups. The main group attacked a camp near the Little Bighorn River in June, 1876, without waiting for reinforcements that were on their way. Within an hour, all 262 soldiers and attached personnel of the 7th cavalry were wiped out.

A warrior's weapons and battle regalia

What weapons did Plains warriors carry?

When they went on a raid, they took bows, arrows, a lance, and a shield to protect them from the lances and arrows of the enemy. They might also carry a club with a sharpened stone at the end, a tomahawk, or a knife.

Government forces were sometimes defeated by Native Americans.

Were there any women warriors?

There certainly were! Running Eagle was a famous female Blackfeet warrior who led others into battle. Buffalo Calf Road Woman was equally renowned among the Cheyenne. The Lakota (Sioux) and Crow also had a tradition of including female warriors in their raiding parties.

Who was the War Woman?

The Cherokee did not go to war without first holding a special meeting to discuss the matter. At this meeting the opinion of the community's women was represented by their spokesperson—and she was called the War Woman. The fate of captured enemies was also decided by Cherokee women.

Many Native American women were sharp shooters and able horsewomen.

Which tribes were almost wiped out by Kit Carson?

The Mescaleros, and then the Navajo, were attacked and rounded up by Colonel Kit Carson in the 1860s, during the Civil War. Those who were not killed were forced onto poor reservations, where many died.

Who said: "Always remember that your father never sold his country"?

Chief Joseph of the Nez Perce said this to his sons shortly before he died in 1871. A treaty robbing the tribe of its best land had been forced on his people. Chief Joseph wanted his children to know that he had never agreed to it. After his death, war broke out between the Nez Perce and government troops.

Who did the Native Americans call Long Hair?

Long Hair was General Custer, the officer in charge of the U.S. Army at the battle of the Little Bighorn. The name came from Custer's habit of letting his gold-colored hair grow long—though shortly before the battle he had it cut shorter than usual.

Where was the Trail of Tears?

It started in the Carolinas and Georgia and ended in Oklahoma. The discovery of gold in Georgia made the presence of Native Americans there unwelcome to the whites. In 1838, some 16,000 Cherokees were rounded up by the army and forced at the point of bayonets to trek northwest to new land. The trek, which lasted throughout a cold winter and covered roughly 1,000 miles (1,600 km), became known as the Trail of Tears. When it was over, it was estimated that more than 4,000 people had died.

Who was captured dishonorably but died honorably?

Osceola, a chief of the Seminoles in Florida. He was tricked by a false flag of truce and captured in 1837. From a prison bed, dressed in his war outfit, he said farewell to the army officers and his own family, and died peacefully.

How did smallpox affect the Mandans?

The Mandan people lived on the upper Missouri in North Dakota. When they first came into contact with European settlers and traders, they caught smallpox from them. Having no resistance to the disease, it wiped them out (by 1837, there were fewer than 150 Mandan).

7,000 soldiers forced the Cherokee nation to march on the Trail of Tears.

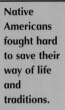

Who died while his arms were held back by a fellow Native American?

Chief Crazy Horse, who had the greatest military record of any Sioux that fought the U.S. Army. He was feared by the white soldiers and envied by other chiefs. Arrested at the age of 35, he was bayoneted to death by a soldier, while his arms were held by the traitor Little Big Man.

What did Young Chief Joseph say when his people were surrounded and outnumbered by the army?

He said these famous words: "I want to have time to look for my children and see how many I can find. Maybe I shall find them among the dead. Hear me, my chiefs, I am tired. My heart is sick and sad. From where the Sun now stands, I will fight no more forever."

Which state declared that the Cherokee nation did not exist?

The state of Georgia. Georgia declared Cherokees did not exist so it could forbid them from digging for gold, which had been discovered there. Georgia also made it illegal for Native Americans to testify in court, because they were not Christians.

Native Americans fought hard to save their way of life and traditions.

Whose brave hearts were buried at Wounded Knee?

Men, women, and children of the Lakota (Sioux) were massacred in 1890 at Wounded Knee Creek near Pine Ridge, South Dakota. It happened after a Ghost Dance (a ritual dance wishing back the good days before the whites came), when the Lakota people who surrendered were rounded up by the army. A tense situation developed and shooting broke out. A famous book about the event is entitled *Bury My Heart At Wounded Knee*.

Who was captured only 30 miles (48 km) from safety?

In an attempt to escape the U.S. Army in 1877, two Native American chiefs—Young Chief Joseph and Chief Looking Glass—led their people on a 1,600-mile (2,600 km) trek from Oregon to Montana. They and their people were captured just before reaching safety in Canada.

Did Sitting Bull defeat Custer?

No, Chief Sitting Bull was not even present at the battle. Battle honors belong to Gall, the Hunkpapa Sioux leader, and to Chief Crazy Horse. Sitting Bull helped to unite the tribes to fight against the army, which was determined to move them off their land and onto reservations. He led his people to safety in Canada after the battle was over, but the shortage of buffalo (after the Great Buffalo slaughter of 1880) meant they had little to eat. In 1881 he surrendered at Fort Buford in Montana.

Catlin painted 470 paintings of Native Americans.

Did Longfellow's Hiawatha really exist?

Yes, Hiawatha was a Mohawk Indian who supported the formation of the Iroquois Confederacy. This union of five tribes into one democratic body was the idea of the spiritual leader, Dekanawida.

Who painted Native American chiefs?

George Catlin (1796–1872) was a painter who traveled west in the 1800s. He painted unique portraits of chiefs and Native American life, including buffalo and moose hunts. His paintings of chiefs, such as Chief Osceola, are world famous.

What did Sequoyah invent for his people?

A written language for his Cherokee people. Sequoyah (1776–1843) realized that a written constitution and permanent records would help strengthen the position of the Cherokee people. The first Native American newspaper appeared in Cherokee in 1828.

Who was Sarah Winnemucca?

She was a Paiute woman, born in 1844, who learned to read and write and educated herself. She became a translator and a go-between for her own people and the government. She later wrote her own life story, telling how white people changed the Paiute way of life.

Who was the greatest Apache warrior?

Geronimo, whose first wife and three children were murdered by Mexicans. Born in 1829, he led the fight against invaders of Apache land in the 1860s. He was caught only once, and boasted famously to the army: "Why I tell you that you are a liar right in the midst of your troops is that you have never caught me shooting." He surrendered in 1886 and died in prison in 1909.

Who was Cochise?

He was a fierce chief of the Chiricahuas, an Apache tribe of the Arizona area. He made peace with General Howard of the U.S. Army after Howard entered his camp unarmed. He stayed loyal to the terms of the treaty until he died three years later in 1874.

What was Pocahontas famous for?

She was famous for pleading for the life of Captain John Smith, an English settler in Virginia captured by the Powhatan people in 1607. She was later kidnapped by the English, and adapted to their way of life, marrying an Englishman in 1914. She died in England.

The battle at Little Bighorn took place on June 25–26, 1876.

How did Washakie help the U.S. Army?

Washakie (1798–1900) was a Shoshone who helped establish a successful reservation for his people. Trusted by the white authorities, he encouraged the Shoshone to act as scouts for the U.S. Army. The army honored him by renaming one of their forts in Wyoming Fort Washakie.

Do pow-wows still happen?

Pow-wows—originally gatherings of Native American spiritual leaders—first started among Plains people, but have now spread to the southwest. Over 1,000 pow-wows took place each year in the 1990s. These social festivals celebrate a vibrant cultural life.

Who helped build the Empire State Building?

In the 1880s, Mohawks were hired to work on the steel girders being erected to support a Canadian railroad bridge. By the 1930s, when many skyscrapers were being built in New York, Mohawk construction workers were well-known for their fearless ability to work at great heights. The Empire State Building is just one of the structures they helped to build. The Mohawk tradition of high-rise building is still alive today.

What happened at Wounded Knee in 1973?

The American Indian Movement seized armed control of Wounded Knee for 71 days in protest against a history of ill-treatment by the whites. The leader of the protest movement, Russell Means, later played a role in the 1992 film *The Last of the Mohicans*.

Traditions such as the Pueblo Indians' Turkey Dance live on.

Are Native Americans becoming extinct?

Not at all, though it was once thought they would become extinct or simply marry into the rest of the United States. But did you know that Native Americans form only about 1% of the U.S. population? They occupy more space in the imagination of the United States than they do land! In the 1970s, they went to court and settled important claims to do with territory. Today, their cultural traditions are stronger than at any time in the last 100 years.

Today, the Apache way of life continues in places like Arizona.

What is a Peacemaker's Court?

It is a modern revival of traditional Navajo justice. It started in about 1982, and operates in seven courtrooms in Navajo communities. Peacemakers, not judges, listen to a dispute and decide on compensation that will satisfy both sides in the argument.

When did a president visit a Native American reservation?

In July 1999, President Clinton visited the Pine Ridge Reservation in South Dakota, scene of the Wounded Knee massacre in 1890. It was the first visit by a U.S. president for 60 years.

Where can the "Lost Colony" be found?

In North Carolina, where a settlement was founded in the 1580s. Settlers moved in, but their supply ship was unable to return for three years, by which time the colony had vanished. Their descendants are thought by some to be the Lumbee people, who still live in North Carolina today.

Who never surrendered, but made peace in 1962?

The Mikasukis people fled to the swamplands of Florida over 150 years ago. From there, they continued to insist that they were at war with the United States and its army. Finally, in 1962, they signed a peace treaty.

What are the moving words of a modern Pueblo prayer?

"Hold onto what is good, even if it is a handful of earth. Hold onto what you believe, even if it is a tree that stands alone. Hold onto what you must do, even if it is a long way from home."

Pilgrims

What did John White draw?

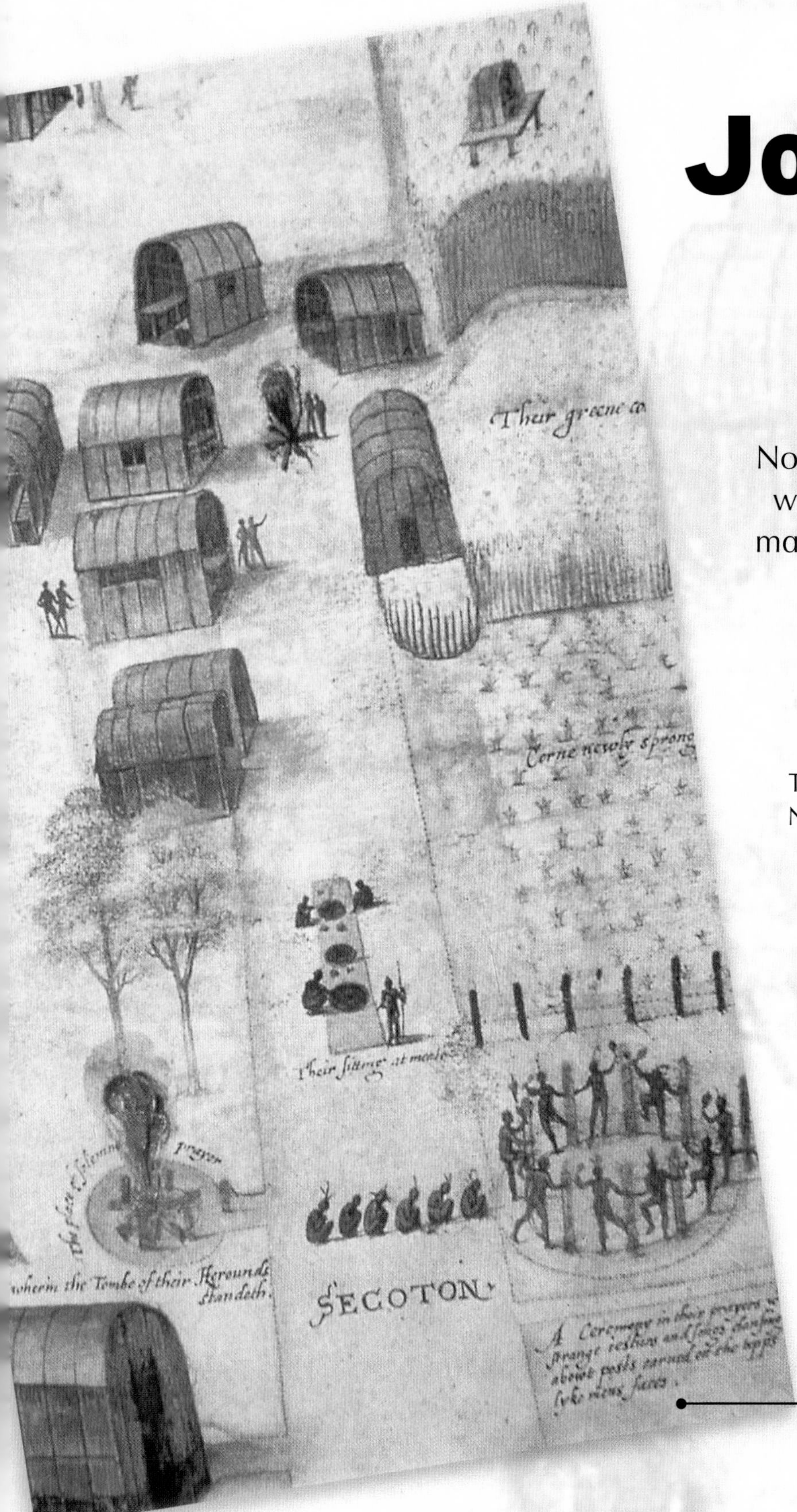

In 1585, an expedition landed at Roanoke Island (in present-day North Carolina). One of the members was an artist named John White. He made many sketches and watercolors of the animals and plants that he saw there, and of the Native Americans that he met.

Who "found" Newfoundland?

The Vikings were the first Europeans to reach North America, sailing there from Greenland about 1000 CE. Nearly five hundred years then passed before an Italian sailor named John Cabot landed in North America, in 1497. His ship was the *Matthew*, and his voyage was paid for by England's King Henry VII. Like Christopher Columbus before him, Cabot thought that he was sailing to Asia—the land of spices and riches. He landed probably somewhere in present-day Newfoundland. Nearly a century later, in 1583, the Englishman Sir Humphrey Gilbert sailed across the Atlantic and claimed Newfoundland as an English territory on behalf of Queen Elizabeth I.

Their greene co

Corne newly sprong

Their sitting at meate

the place of solemne prayer

wherin the Tombe of their Herounds standeth

SECOTON

A Ceremonye in their prayers with strange restures and songes dansing about postes carved on the topps lyke mens faces

John White's illustrations give an idea of what Native American life was like in the 1500s.

The Iroquois were based around the Great Lakes and lived in longhouses like these.

What riches did Cabot find by the basketful?

Cabot did not bring back exotic spices and fabulous jewels from his voyage of 1497. But he did bring news of waters teeming with fish off the coast of Newfoundland. There were so many fish in the sea that they could be caught by lowering baskets weighted with stones over the side of the ship. Soon, fishermen from England, France, Italy, Portugal, and Spain were visiting these waters and sailing home with huge loads of fish.

What happened to the "Lost Colony"?

In 1587, Sir Walter Raleigh organized a second expedition to the New World. The colonists on the expedition were intending to settle on the mainland in the Chesapeake area, but the crossing took longer than expected and the captain refused to sail farther than Roanoke Island. There the colonists landed. Due to the war between England and Spain, no further voyages were made until 1590, when the artist John White sailed once again to Roanoke to join the colonists. But they had disappeared and no trace of them was ever found.

Who were the first settlers to spend a winter in the New World?

In April 1585, a small fleet of five large and two smaller ships left England under the command of Richard Grenville. The expedition was organized by Sir Walter Raleigh. Its aim was to set up a base for English warships at Roanoke Island. But the waters around the island were found to be too shallow for warships and, after one winter on the island, the colonists returned to England.

What was the message carved on the tree?

When John White arrived on Roanoke Island in 1590 hoping to find the colonists of the 1587 expedition, all he found was the word CROATOAN carved on a tree. The Croatan were Native Americans from a neighboring island, and were known to be friendly toward European settlers. However, storms prevented White from getting to their island, so he never discovered the fate of the missing settlers.

Where did Jacques Cartier sail to?

Jacques Cartier was a sailor from St. Malo in France. Backed financially by the French king Francis I, he made three expeditions in 1534, 1535, and 1541–42. Cartier explored the Gulf of St. Lawrence and the St. Lawrence River as far as present-day Montreal.

Who founded Quebec?

A group of French explorers led by Samuel de Champlain sailed to North America in 1608 and made their way up the St. Lawrence River. They set up a fur trading post and named it Quebec. Only eight of the 24 colonists survived the first winter there, but Quebec went on to become the first settlement of New France.

Who were the Jamestown adventurers?

The men who sailed across the ocean to settle Jamestown were a mixed bunch. They included soldiers, laborers, craftsmen, a doctor, a priest, and several well-off gentlemen. Most had come hoping to make their fortunes in the New World, and they soon set about exploring the area in the hope of finding gold and other treasures.

Where did three ships find a permanent home?

After a journey across the Atlantic Ocean lasting about four months, 105 men in three ships sailed up the James River in Virginia and looked for somewhere to land. The year was 1607. Their ships were owned by the London Company, and their task was to find a natural harbor that would be safe from attack by England's enemy, the Spanish. When they found a good place, the adventurers began building simple shelters there. They called their new settlement Jamestown. It was the first permanent English settlement in North America.

Jamestown was the site of the first successful British settlement in America.

Did the Native Americans help the settlers?

The Native Americans of the Jamestown area were Algonquian-speakers, led by a chief named Powhatan. At first the Powhatans were suspicious of the settlers, but they soon began to help them with supplies of food. Later, when the Powhatans realized that the newcomers intended to take over their land, they attacked the colony, burning crops and killing livestock.

What happened to Pocahontas?

In 1613, one of the daughters of Chief Powhatan was kidnapped by the European colonists. She was named Pocahontas. While in captivity, Pocahontas and a tobacco farmer named John Rolfe fell in love, and the pair got married. This was the first marriage between a settler and a Native American, and it helped to strengthen good relations between the two peoples.

Pocahontas became a Christian and changed her name to Rebecca before she married John Rolfe.

What treasure did English adventurers hope to find in the New World?

Gold! In the reign of Queen Elizabeth I, many great English sailors roamed the seas. Sir Francis Drake was the first Englishman to sail around the world. Sir Walter Raleigh was the first to organize colonies of settlers in America. These sea captains were privateers—with the permission of their queen, they attacked and looted enemy ships, returning in triumph with their plunder. They also brought back tales of untold riches and of a city named El Dorado that was made of gold. These stories inspired many adventurers to try their luck in the New World.

How many settlers survived their first winter abroad?

Out of the 105 settlers who landed in April 1607, only 38 were still alive after their first winter in the colony. Many died from diseases such as typhoid, malaria, and dysentery; others died from starvation. Only the arrival of more settlers in 1608 and 1609 saved the colony from dying out.

Why did the settlers grow tobacco?

The colonists did not find gold, but they did discover a crop that grew well in Virginia, and which they could sell in England for a profit. The crop was tobacco. In 1612, a settler named John Rolfe first introduced to Virginia tobacco plants brought from the Caribbean, and a year later the first shipload of leaves was sent back to England from America.

Why was food scarce?

The Jamestown settlers often argued among themselves about the running of the colony. As the first winter drew in, they realized that they had not grown enough crops to provide sufficient food. This was mainly because so many men had deserted the fields to look for gold. The colony would not have survived its first winter without food from the Powhatans.

Who was John Smith?

After the disastrous first winter, it took a strong man to pull the colony through the following year. This man was a soldier named John Smith. He ruled with an iron fist, forcing the settlers to plant crops, and build houses and defenses.

How were Pilgrim children different?

The Pilgrims disapproved of the relaxed way that Dutch children were brought up, with freedom to play. The children of Pilgrim families wore plain clothes, were treated strictly, and were expected to be seen and not heard.

Who were the Pilgrims?

In November 1620, a group of men, women, and children put ashore on the rocky coastline of New England. Like the first settlers of Jamestown, they had come to start a new life in the New World—but the reasons for their voyage were very different. They had come to seek not gold, but the freedom to follow their religion without persecution. They became known as the Pilgrims.

Pilgrims believed that devotion to God could be shown only through worship, not by the clothes they wore. They dressed very simply.

What is Scrooby?

Scrooby, a small village in Nottinghamshire, England, was the center of the Nonconformist Church of the Pilgrims. Several Pilgrim leaders came from Scrooby, including John Robinson, William Brewster, and William Bradford.

Why did the Pilgrims flee England for the Netherlands ?

In 1608, a group of English Nonconformists fled to the Netherlands to escape religious persecution. It was a risky move, because the punishment for illegal emigration was prison. But the reward was the freedom to worship as they wanted.

What happened to the women and children?

In 1607, the Pilgrims, led by William Brewster and John Robinson, made their first attempt to flee to the Netherlands. But the captain of the ship they were planning to sail on robbed them, and the attempt failed. A year later the Pilgrims tried again. This time the men went aboard ahead of the women and children to check that there was no trap, only to see their families on shore being rounded up by the authorities. The men had to sail without them, and many months passed before they were reunited in the Netherlands.

Many Pilgrim women were expert weavers. First they spun the wool into yarn on spinning wheels.

Where did the Pilgrims first learn to weave?

At first the Pilgrims who had fled England lived in Amsterdam, the capital of the Netherlands. After a short time, however, they moved to the university town of Leiden, where many got jobs as weavers.

What was a Nonconformist?

In the late 1500s and early 1600s, some people broke away from the Catholic and Anglican Churches because they did not like the pomp and ceremony of church services, and did not believe that you needed a priest to help you to talk to God. They worshiped solemnly in simple surroundings, and because they did not conform to the established religions, they were called Nonconformists.

What was the Pilgrim Press?

It was a printing machine set up in Leiden by William Brewster. The press was used to print pamphlets about the Nonconformist Church. The pamphlets were distributed in the Netherlands and, illegally, in England.

Why did the Pilgrims decide to leave the Netherlands?

The Pilgrims did not feel at home in the Netherlands. They did not want to follow a Dutch way of life or learn the Dutch language. Many Pilgrims began to talk about going to America and carving out a new life in an entirely new land.

What was the Mayflower?

The second ship that the Pilgrims chose for their voyage to the New World was named the *Mayflower*. In 1620, it sailed from London to Southampton, on England's south coast, where it met up with the *Speedwell*. The two ships set sail together for the New World in August 1620, but were forced to turn back because the *Speedwell* was leaking badly. A second attempt also failed, and the ships were forced to dock in Plymouth. The Pilgrims decided to abandon the *Speedwell*, and all crowded onto the *Mayflower*. The *Mayflower* left Plymouth on September 16, 1620.

This illustration shows a reconstruction of the Mayflower in full sail.

Why could the Pilgrims not land when they reached the shore?

When the excited Pilgrims saw land, they were desperate to leave their damp and dirty quarters and go ashore. But it was many days before the ship's captain could find a safe place to drop anchor. The Pilgrims first set foot in America at Cape Cod, in present-day Provincetown, Massachusetts.

Who kept a journal of the voyage?

One of the organizers of the expedition to the New World was a man named William Bradford. He wrote a journal recording the adventures of the Pilgrims on the crossing. He also listed every man, woman, and child aboard the *Mayflower*. From his list we know that there were 24 households, as well as some single men. Bradford later became governor of the Pilgrims' new settlement.

The *Mayflower* was a three-masted carrack ship.

What did the Pilgrims take with them?

The Pilgrims were going to start a new life in the New World, so they packed as much as they could into the *Mayflower's* holds. They took tools, seeds, and livestock with them, and many families also took their dogs. They also needed to provide for themselves while at sea, so each family had its own bedding and cooking equipment.

How big was the *Mayflower*?

The *Mayflower* was a small ship to face the dangers of an Atlantic crossing. It was about 90 ft (27m) long, and weighed about 180 tons. With 102 passengers aboard, as well as the ship's crew and all their belongings, conditions were extremely cramped.

What happened to the *Mayflower*?

The master of the *Mayflower*, Captain Jones, and his crew spent the first winter in the Pilgrims' new colony. It was not until the following April (1621) that the *Mayflower* set off on its return journey to England. It reached London in May, bringing the first news of the Pilgrims' safe arrival to friends and relations back home.

Was the crossing a good one?

No! It took the *Mayflower* 64 days to sail from Plymouth, England, across the Atlantic to within sight of the New World. The voyage was rough and stormy, and at one point it looked as if the ship might break apart. The wretched Pilgrims were thrown about helplessly in their cramped quarters, and many were continually seasick.

What other names were given to the Pilgrims?

The people who arrived in America on the *Mayflower* are also known as the "Forefathers," the "First Comers," and the "Old Stock."

What argument ended in a compact?

As the *Mayflower* sailed up and down the coastline of Cape Cod looking for somewhere to land, the Pilgrims on board started arguing. Some simply wanted to get off the ship, no matter where; others wanted to sail on and look for a really good landing place, close to other settlements. Some of the Pilgrims threatened to break from the group and set out alone, but in the end they all agreed it would be better to stay together. They drew up a document laying down the laws and aims of the new colony. This document has become known as the Mayflower Compact. It was signed on board the *Mayflower* by 41 of the male Pilgrims on November 21, 1620.

As the Pilgrims had no royal charter, they established government by signing the Mayflower Compact.

When did the Pilgrims found New Plymouth?

A small expedition of Pilgrims from the *Mayflower* decided on the site of New Plymouth on December 21, 1620. They returned to the *Mayflower* with the good news, and a few days later everything was prepared for the final stage of the *Mayflower's* journey—a distance of about 24 miles (40 km).

Who was the first governor of the colony?

After signing the Mayflower Compact, the Pilgrims elected a governor for their new colony. His name was John Carver, and he was so well-liked and respected that he was reelected in March 1621. Sadly, he died a few weeks later, one of the last victims of the epidemic that claimed many Pilgrims' lives.

Did anyone give up and go home with the *Mayflower*?

No. Amazingly, despite the hardships of the winter, the surviving Pilgrims were determined to stay in the new colony, and none returned with the *Mayflower* when it departed for England in April 1621.

Why were the fields deserted?

The Pilgrims settled on a site that had been cleared and farmed by people before. But the fields were deserted. The Pilgrims learned later that an epidemic, brought by earlier settlers, had killed most of the Native American inhabitants of this settlement, known as Pawtuxet, just two years earlier.

The Plymouth colony named their settlement after the English town from which they had sailed.

How did a shallop help find a place to settle?

After signing the Mayflower Compact, a group of men went ashore to collect firewood and find a spring with fresh drinking water. Meanwhile, on board ship, the crew and some Pilgrims began to put together the small boat, named a shallop, that had been brought for exploring the coastline. It took many days to rebuild the shallop, but when it was ready, the Pilgrims took it in turns to look for a place to settle. They finally found somewhere with a safe harbor, several freshwater streams, and some abandoned fields. They called the place New Plymouth.

How did the Pilgrims celebrate their first Christmas?

The Pilgrims arrived at their new home in the middle of winter. First they needed to build some kind of shelter so that families, stores, and equipment could be moved off the *Mayflower*. They spent Christmas Eve in prayer, but on Christmas Day it was business as usual—felling trees and cutting logs for building.

How many Pilgrims survived the first winter?

After the rough ocean crossing, many of the Pilgrims were in poor health when they arrived. Ashore, life continued to be hard, and during the first winter nearly half the group died.

Who gave the Pilgrims help?

Native Americans had lived off the land for many centuries, and were generous with their advice to the Pilgrims. They showed them how to plant the corn they had taken from an abandoned store the previous winter, and taught them new ways of cooking, farming, and fishing.

At first the Pilgrims and many Native Americans shared the land in harmony.

What was Squanto's unusual story?

Squanto was an English-speaking Native American. Originally from the Pawtuxet tribe, he was kidnapped by the adventurer Captain Hunt and taken to London as a slave. But he managed to escape and return home. Squanto gave invaluable help to the Pilgrims, acting as an interpreter between them and the local Native Americans.

Who surprised the Pilgrims?

All that first winter, the Pilgrims were uneasily aware of the presence of Native Americans all around them. But, beset by sickness and the need to build shelters and to hunt and fish for food, the settlers had little time to build defenses against possible attacks from hostile people. Then, in mid-March, as the Pilgrims were holding a meeting to discuss how to defend themselves, a Native American strode into their settlement. His name was Samoset, and he was the Sagamore (subordinate chief) of an Abenaki tribe. This was the Pilgrims' first contact with the local people of the area.

What was Samoset's warning?

Samoset warned the Pilgrims to beware of the Nauset tribe, who lived to the northeast of New Plymouth. The Nausets had reason to be hostile to Europeans, for only recently an English adventurer named Thomas Hunt had kidnapped several Nausets and Pawtuxets, and taken them off to be sold as slaves.

What did Samoset tell the Pilgrims?

Samoset had spent some time with the Europeans who fished along the coast, and knew enough phrases to be able to communicate with the Pilgrims. He told them about the geography of the coast to the north of New Plymouth, and that the place where they had settled had once belonged to the Pawtuxet tribe.

How did some stolen corn save the colony?

The small groups of Pilgrims who left the *Mayflower* to search for a suitable landing place came across many signs of the Native Americans who had lived there. They unearthed some graves, filled with precious objects, which they quickly covered over again. They also found Native American stores full of corn. The Pilgrims knew that they needed all the food they could get for the winter, so they helped themselves to as much corn as they could carry. In fact, the stolen corn provided them with seed to plant the following spring and, without it, the new colony probably would not have survived.

Who drew up a peace treaty?

The most important negotiations in the early days of the colony were held between Governor John Carver and Massasoit, the Grand Sachem (intertribal chief) of the Wampanoag tribe. With the help of the interpreter, Squanto, Carver and Massasoit drew up a peace treaty. The Pilgrims provided meat and brandy for the chief. In return, Massasoit gave them gifts of tobacco.

What was a house-raising?

When they first arrived in the New World, the settlers built shelters as quickly as possible from whatever materials came to hand. These simple homes were often made from wattles (woven frames) and sticks, plastered over with mud. The roofs were thatched with grass. Once a settlement was established, the colonists started to build more permanent houses. These were made of wood, and several families would work together to help with sawing tree trunks and setting heavy timbers into the ground. "House-raising" soon became a community occasion, with the owner providing food and drink for the other settlers who came to help.

Why were the colonists afraid of the forests?

The first settlers in the New World were amazed at the thick forests that covered much of the land. It was easy to get lost in these forests, and the colonists were always fearful of attack from hostile Native Americans. At first they avoided going into the woods as much as possible. But later they used the forests as a valuable source of timber for building and game for eating.

What do we remember at Thanksgiving today?

In the U.S. and Canada, Thanksgiving is celebrated every year, in remembrance of the Pilgrims' first harvest. In the U.S. it is celebrated on the fourth Thursday of November; in Canada on the second Monday of October.

As the settlers grew used to their surroundings, they were able to build better homes, which afforded them more protection.

Who ate five deer at Thanksgiving?

In the fall of 1621, the Pilgrims harvested their first crops in the New World. In the spring they had planted barley, peas, and the Native Americans' corn. The corn had grown well, although the barley and peas were less successful. The Pilgrims held a feast to give thanks for this store of food, which was enough to see them through the winter. Grand Sachem Massasoit and about 90 of his Wampanoag tribe came to share the Pilgrims' feast, bringing five deer with them. This was the first Thanksgiving.

Thanksgiving began as a celebration of the first harvest.

Who planted fish?

The early settlers noticed that near rivers or the ocean, the Native Americans placed dead fish beneath their corn plants in the spring. Realizing that the fish acted as a natural fertiliser that made the corn grow strong, the settlers followed the Native Americans' example.

Was the New World a land of plenty?

Yes! There were fish in the ocean and rivers, many wild berries and plants that were good for eating, and large quantities of game such as deer, ducks, and geese. There was also shellfish, such as oysters and clams, along the seashore.

Who carried boats on their heads?

One of the easiest ways to get around in the New World was by water, along the great rivers that flowed into the Atlantic Ocean. The colonists copied the way the Native Americans made their canoes from long strips of birch bark. These light craft could easily be carried around rapids or waterfalls.

Who ate the passenger?

The colonists were astonished by the numbers of pigeons that flew in the skies of the New World. These birds were passenger pigeons, and their huge flocks sometimes blacked out the entire sky. They were very easy to catch for food—so easy that by 1900 they were extinct in the wild (and in 1914 the last captive bird died).

Which crops did the settlers grow?

The first settlers who came to the New World from Europe brought with them seeds of the crops they grew at home, such as wheat. But they found that one of the best crops for the soil and climate of the Northeast was the corn grown by the Native Americans, and this became an important crop for the colonists.

Who was brought back to life?

One day, word came to the Pilgrims that Massasoit, the chief of the local Wampanoag tribe, was dying. Massasoit had been a good friend to the Pilgrims, so Governor Bradford decided to send him medicine. After drinking the herbal remedies prepared by the Pilgrims, Massasoit recovered.

What was chief Massasoit's warning?

To thank the Pilgrims for their help, Massasoit warned them about a planned raid. He had forbidden his own tribe to take part, but he knew that other tribes were about to attack Plymouth and a neighboring settlement set up by the English adventurers.

Massasoit's statue is a tribute to the Native Americans who supported the Pilgrims during difficult times.

What did *Fortune* bring in 1621?

The Pilgrims had lived in the New World for one year when an unexpected arrival took the small colony by surprise. In November 1621, a ship sailed into Plymouth harbor. Fearing that it might be an enemy ship, the Pilgrims ran to grab their weapons—but it was the *Fortune* carrying a second wave of colonists. Joyfully, the Pilgrims ran to the shore to greet the new arrivals.

What good news did the *Fortune* bring?

The *Fortune* brought news and letters from friends and family at home—the first communication with the outside world since the Pilgrims had arrived in the New World.

...and what about the bad news?

The Pilgrims' expedition on the *Fortune* had been very badly planned. There was barely enough food on board to keep the new settlers alive during the crossing. To the horror of the original colonists in Plymouth, the new settlers had brought no supplies or equipment with them. The number of extra mouths to feed brought the colony close to starvation that winter.

What happened to the Pilgrims?

The Pilgrims suffered Native American attacks, starvation, and illness, but their colony survived. As more settlers arrived in New England, trade increased and the Pilgrims became more prosperous. But their colony remained small, and in the 1690s it was taken over by the larger and more powerful colony of Massachusetts.

New arrivals landing at Plymouth without supplies placed an extra strain on already limited food supplies.

Who came unprepared?

Two shiploads of adventurers from England arrived in 1622, just as the settlers were close to starvation. The new arrivals brought no supplies with them, and relied on the Pilgrims' goodwill and hospitality. When the newcomers finally left to set up their own colony, they left behind their sick for the Pilgrims to nurse back to health.

Who got ambushed by pirates?

The colonists loaded the *Fortune* with trade goods—beaver skins and roughly sawn timber—to be sold in England. The ship set sail in December 1621, but on its return journey across the Atlantic, it was captured by French pirates. They stole the Pilgrims' precious cargo and delayed the arrival of their letters in England.

How many more Pilgrims came to Plymouth?

In the years that followed, two more ships arrived with Pilgrim settlers from the Netherlands and England. In 1623, the *Anne* sailed into Plymouth harbor carrying about 60 Pilgrims. A few days later, a small ship named the *Little James* also arrived, for the Pilgrims to use for trade along the coast of North America. Finally, in 1630, the *Handmaid* brought another 60 Pilgrims. These were the last arrivals to be able to call themselves the "Pilgrim Fathers of New England."

Who were the Puritans?

The Puritans were Nonconformists who disapproved of the Anglican Church. They dressed soberly in simple clothes, and they led a pure life without entertainments. In the new colonies, Governor Winthrop banned theatrical performances and drinking. Everyone had to go to church.

Who were the Quakers?

The Quakers were a group of English Nonconformists who followed the teaching of a preacher named George Fox. In the early 1680s, a group of Quakers, organized by William Penn, set sail for America. Penn settled an area to the west of the Delaware River, establishing the state of Pennsylvania.

Like other Nonconformists, Quakers were persecuted for their beliefs.

Why did New Amsterdam become New York?

English settlers were not the only European colonizers arriving in the New World. In 1625, a small group of settlers from the Netherlands set up a trading post on Manhattan Island, calling it New Amsterdam. The colonists found that the land on Manhattan was good for growing crops, and the settlement flourished. In 1664, the Dutch colony was attacked and captured by English forces, and its name was changed to New York, after the town of York in England.

What was the largest expedition to the New World ?

In March 1630, a fleet of 11 ships left England for America. On board were nearly 1,000 men, women, and children. This massive expedition was organized by the Massachusetts Bay Company. Its leader was John Winthrop, a Puritan landowner from Suffolk in eastern England. Even before he sailed, Winthrop had been elected governor of the new colony. When the settlers arrived in the New World, they chose a site near the Charles River and named it Boston, after the town in Lincolnshire from where many of them had come.

Were the Puritans well prepared?

Yes. The Puritan settlers knew what to take with them from letters sent home by the Pilgrims. They filled their ships with tools and livestock. Within a very short time, they had set up 11 towns around the Boston area.

Did everyone follow the Puritan way of life?

No! Many settlers were not Puritans and did not like the Puritan way of life. Some of them formed breakaway colonies. Roger Williams, who founded Rhode Island, was banished from the Massachusetts colony for disagreeing with its leaders.

How many families were needed to start a town?

Towns grew up amazingly quickly as more and more settlers arrived in Massachusetts. A group of about 20 families would join together to found a new town. Once they had been granted land, they would lay out a village street with a simple church at its center. A plot of land next to the church was reserved for the minister's house. Areas of about one acre were marked out for the other homes.

Who named a colony after the Virgin Mary?

The Pilgrims were not the only people to suffer religious persecution in England. When King Henry VIII established the Anglican Church in the 1500s, Roman Catholics were prevented from worshiping as they wanted. In 1633, two ships sailed for America carrying Catholic settlers. They founded a colony and called it Maryland.

How many more settlers arrived?

John Winthrop's expedition of 1630 was followed by many ships full of settlers from England. Over the next 10 years, thousands more people arrived in America to settle in New England. Many of them were Puritans or were sympathetic to the Puritan way of life.

A New England kitchen contained objects brought from Europe as well as newly crafted utensils.

As relations between Native Americans and settlers became strained, armed forces were set up in settlements.

Why did friendship turn to warfare?

At the start, settlers and Native Americans were often friendly to each other. The Native Americans helped the newcomers with supplies and know-how for their survival as they struggled to set up their colonies. In return, the settlers gave them goods that they did not produce for themselves, such as pots and pans, knives, blankets, guns, and alcohol. As the settlers took over more land and became more threatening, the Native Americans grew more hostile. Sometimes there was open warfare.

Who encouraged tribal warfare?

Many colonies did their best to encourage bad feelings between tribes. The European settlers knew that if the Native American peoples were busy fighting each other, they would be less likely to attack the colonists.

How did the colonists defend themselves?

One of the first things that European settlers did when they arrived in America was to protect themselves against possible Native American attack. They spent a lot of time and effort building forts, and set up armed forces called militias. Captain Myles Standish was the leader of the Pilgrims' first militia.

Who was King Philip?

After the death of the Native American chief Massasoit in 1662, his son Metacomet became chief. The colonists called him "Philip" or "King Philip." Because the colonists were taking land from him, Metacomet was not as friendly toward them as his father had been. From 1675 to 1676 he led his people against them in a war that became known as King Philip's War.

Who was shot in a swamp?

Chief Metacomet was finally trapped and shot in a swamp. King Philip's War was a disaster for the Native American population. Thousands died, leaving much of the coastal regions of northeast America clear for the Europeans to move into.

Why did the Native Americans fall sick?

As more and more European settlers poured into America, the Native Americans who had lived there for generations began to suffer badly, and in many ways. Probably their worst enemy was both silent and invisible. European settlers brought illnesses with them that were entirely new to the Native Americans, who had no resistance to diseases such as smallpox. Thousands of Native Americans died as epidemics swept through their tribes in the 1600s.

King Philip enlisted the help of other Native American tribes in his struggle against the settlers.

Who died in the massacres of 1622?

By 1622, the colony in Virginia had expanded to cover a 100-mile (160-km) stretch along the James River. The local Native Americans realized that they were losing their land and that their way of life was threatened. They attacked the colonists and massacred some 350 settlers. Many Native Americans died in the revenge attacks that followed.

How many died from European diseases?

It is very difficult to know exactly how many Native Americans were living in northeastern America before the arrival of the European settlers. Some historians believe that, in 1600, the area of New England was home to about 25,000 Native Americans. It is likely that more than half of this number died from diseases in the 20 years after the first settlers arrived.

What was the Pequot War?

This was the first large-scale battle between Native Americans and settlers in the northeast. The Pequots had moved east, threatening both the local tribes and the European colonists. In 1637, the English settlers attacked the Pequots and wiped out almost the entire tribe.

What started the American Revolution?

When was the Declaration of Independence?

The American colonists declared themselves independent from Britain on July 4th, 1776. But it wasn't until 1783 that Britain recognized the independence of the United States of America. Until then, the fighting continued.

During the 1760s and 1770s, the government in Britain imposed a series of taxes on the colonists in America. The colonists had no representatives in the British parliament and therefore no one to argue their objections. In 1775, the colonists' resentment boiled over into armed resistance—the beginning of the American Revolution.

When did the first Africans arrive in North America?

In about 1619, early settlers in Virginia sailed to Africa to bring back captives to work on their plantations. This was the beginning of the terrible slave trade.

Colonists became disillusioned with being governed by a far-off country that knew little about their way of life.

Delegates from the 13 colonies signed the Declaration of Independence on July 4th, 1776.

What were the 13 colonies?

Europeans continued to settle the northeast coast of America throughout the late 1600s and early 1700s. By 1733, there were 13 British colonies in North America. They were Connecticut, Delaware, Georgia, Maine, Maryland, Massachusetts, New Hampshire, New Jersey, New York, Pennsylvania, Rhode Island, Vermont, and Virginia. They were all ruled by a government far away in Great Britain—but this situation was soon to change.

What happened at Bunker Hill?

The opening skirmishes of the American Revolution happened at Concord and nearby Lexington in April 1775. The first major battle was at Bunker Hill. The colonists were forced to flee, but not until they had killed or wounded more than 1,000 British soldiers.

Who fought a war over furs?

Ever since the first trappers explored the waterways of northern America, the English and French had fought to control the fur trade, which was making them a great deal of money. The two sides engaged in many small wars, often helped by their Native American allies. But the most bitter struggle began in 1754. The fighting spread to Europe in 1756, and lasted for seven years, until 1763. It became known as the Seven Years' War.

Who won the Seven Years' War?

Great Britain eventually won the war after seven long years. Quebec, the capital of New France, surrendered in 1760. By the end of the war, in 1763, the British had taken over New France and governed the whole of eastern North America.

Which was the last of the 13 colonies to be founded?

Georgia. Its charter was issued in 1732, and the first settlers arrived from England in 1733.

Why did the British demand money from their colonies?

After the Seven Years' War, the British colonists in America no longer feared a French invasion from the north. But the British government decided that their colonies needed a permanent army and navy, and expected the colonies to pay toward the upkeep of these forces.

Who were the "backwoodsmen"?

In the Kentucky forests, pioneers known as "backwoodsmen" cleared land for their crops and built themselves rough houses from logs. They had to be entirely self-sufficient in order to survive.

People living in frontier villages had to be entirely self-sufficient.

Why did people go West?

To claim land. Thousands of people from Europe continued to pour into America. Between 1763 and 1776 alone, up to 150,000 people settled there. More people needed more land, and the government could do nothing to stop them moving westward to find it.

Daniel Boone was captured by the Shawnee during the American Revolution, but escaped and reached Boonesborough in time to save it from the British.

Who drew an invisible line at the Appalachian Mountains?

As the Seven Years' War came to an end and Britain took control of French land in North America, many Native American tribes began to rebel. These Native Americans had long been allies of the French, and did not trust the British. In 1763, after several ferocious battles between Native Americans and British troops, the British government ordered all settlers living west of the Appalachian Mountains to withdraw to the east. It also forbade new settlement west of the mountains. The intention was to leave this land free for the Native Americans.

Where did Daniel Boone cut a trail?

The settlers ignored the ban on exploring west of the Appalachian Mountains. In 1775, a judge named Richard Henderson bought a huge area of land in Kentucky from the Cherokees. He then employed the pioneer Daniel Boone to cut a trail through the Appalachian Mountains to his land. Boone had spent many years exploring the mountains and beyond, and knew the area better than any other settler of the time.

Where did Daniel Boone build a town?

At the end of the Wilderness Road, Boone and his companions built a settlement that they named Boonesborough. It was located near the present-day town of Lexington. Before long, several families had settled around Boonesborough, including the owner of the territory, Judge Henderson.

Who trapped the trapper?

Boone met many Native Americans as he traveled through the mountains and beyond. Often these meetings were hostile, and Boone was taken prisoner. He was set free only after he had given up his few possessions and whatever furs he had managed to trap.

Who walked the Wilderness Road?

The trail cut across the Appalachians by Daniel Boone and his 28 woodsmen became known as the Wilderness Road. It started in Virginia, crossed the mountains at the Cumberland Gap, and ended in Kentucky.

Who followed Boone to the West?

For many years the Wilderness Road was the only practical route through the mountains to Kentucky. Despite its dangers, by 1800 more than 200,000 settlers had used the Wilderness Road to move west.

Who lost his homeland on two occasions?

Boone lost his land in Kentucky because he could not prove his legal right of ownership. In 1799, he led another group of settlers, this time to Missouri. Once again, he lost the land he claimed. Boone died in Missouri in 1820.

How the West was Won

Who lived in the West?

When Europeans first arrived in the "New World" of the Americas, they did not move to an empty continent. The land had been home to millions of Native Americans for a thousand generations or more. There were over 200 different tribes in the West, speaking over 75 different languages. The tribes included the Hopi, Clatsop, Pawnee, Mojave, Nez Perce, Shoshone, Chinook, and Zuni. Each group had its own traditions, customs, and ways of life.

Who lived on the Plateau?

Bordered by the Cascade Range to the west and the Rocky Mountains to the east, the Plateau region was home to tribes such as the Chinook, the Northern Shoshone, the Nez Perce, and the Kutenai. The peoples of the Plateau caught salmon in the Columbia and Fraser rivers and foraged for camas roots and other vegetables.

A tepee like this would have been home to a family of the Crow people. It is decorated with hunting scenes.

Who and what lived on the Great Plains?

The Great Plains extend from the Mississippi River westward to the Rocky Mountains. The endless acres of prairie grass were home to many kinds of animals, particularly buffalo. Native American tribes such as the Pawnee and Crow lived on the Great Plains, following the herds of buffalo, which they depended on for their livelihoods.

Who built houses of bark and reeds?

On the Pacific coast, the Native Americans in California built small shelters from reeds. Others made tepee-like structures from the bark of the redwood tree. Farther north, tribes such as the Nootka and the Haida made sturdy rectangular houses from planks of wood tied together with cords.

What was a potlatch?

A potlatch was a ceremony held by the tribes of the Pacific Northwest such as the Tlingit and Chinook. It was a spectacular occasion during which gifts were exchanged, people dressed in their finest clothes, and there was much feasting and celebration.

How was a tepee made?

A tepee was home for the Native Americans of the Great Plains. Made from a conical framework of poles covered with buffalo hides, it was ideal for the nomadic lifestyle of the Plains' peoples, because it was easy to take down, to transport, and to put up again.

How were shells used?

The tribes along the Pacific coast used the beautiful shells of oysters, clams, and other shellfish as a kind of money. They exchanged shells for goods. Some shells ended up thousands of miles away from the coast, worn as ornaments by people who had never been near the sea.

Where did the West begin?

As the settlers saw it, the Western frontier moved slowly westward with them into North America. In the 1600s, the "West" was anywhere beyond the Appalachian Mountains. To them, it was an unknown and dangerous land. By the early 1800s, European settlement had pushed westward as far as the Mississippi, but beyond that was a wild and unfamiliar country. The expeditions of explorers such as Meriwether Lewis and William Clark, and John C. Frémont gradually opened up this wild land, and by the 1840s, pioneer families were beginning to make the long trek westward to a new land and a new life.

Tribes such as these Zunis were living in the West long before Europeans first arrived.

Who lived in multi-level housing?

The peoples of the hot, dry southwest lived in settlements called pueblos. They used adobe (mud brick) to build large living complexes in which they lived all year round. The tribes of this area included the Zuni, the Acoma, and the Hopi.

What strange sight did the Zunis see?

One day in the summer of 1540, the Zunis looked out from their clifftop town to see a procession approaching across the desert. Most of the people in it were Native Americans, but there were also many paler-faced men wearing metal breastplates and riding creatures never before seen by the Zunis—horses. Leading them was the Spanish conquistador (conqueror) Francisco Vásquez de Coronado.

Who was Francisco Vásquez de Coronado?

Francisco Vásquez de Coronado (1510–1554) was one of the Spanish soldiers who went to the "New World" to seek their fortunes in the 1500s.

What were the Spaniards looking for?

Gold! Coronado and the other conquistadors were searching for the "Seven Cities of Gold"—fabled great cities supposedly dripping in gold, silver, and jewels. Tales of such places had been brought back by conquistadors such as Alvar Núñez Cabeza de Vaca, the first European to reach the American West when he was shipwrecked there in 1528. The Spanish already knew of the great riches seized from the Aztec Empire in Mexico by Hernando Cortés after 1519, and the almost unbelievable wealth plundered from the Incas in South America by Francisco Pizarro after 1532.

Did Coronado find gold in America?

No. Despite spending two years looking for the fabled "Seven Cities of Gold," Coronado and his expedition found only desert, endless plains, and small villages. He returned to Mexico "very sad and very weary, completely worn out...."

Which Europeans first saw the Grand Canyon?

Some members of Coronado's party traveled northwest from the Zuni settlements to search for treasure. Instead of precious metals and jewels, they came across a gorge vast beyond their wildest dreams. They were the first Europeans to see the Grand Canyon.

Where was El Pueblo de Nuestra Señora la Reina de los Angeles?

Today the city with this very long name, which means "the village of our lady the queen of the angels," is better known as Los Angeles. It was founded by a group of pioneers in 1781, and was built in a virtual desert. The settlers used water from the foothills of the Sierra Nevada mountains to grow crops and raise livestock.

These fabulous gold objects were made by the Inca people of Peru.

Which animal changed the lives of the Native Americans?

Before the arrival of Europeans, Native Americans had never before seen a horse. The arrival of the horse transformed life for many Native American peoples. Apache and Navajo warriors were among the first to acquire horses. Herds of horses spread rapidly across the West, and horses were traded from one tribe to another. Soon they were used for transportation, hunting buffalo, and war.

Coronado and his men search for the "Seven Cities of Gold."

What was the silent killer the Europeans brought with them?

Guns and horses may have terrified the Native Americans who first came in contact with Europeans, but the invaders carried with them a far more dangerous threat—disease. The Native Americans had no resistance to European diseases such as smallpox, cholera, measles, and tuberculosis, and sickness spread rapidly through many tribes killing millions of Native Americans.

Who went with Coronado?

The great army of people following Coronado in 1540 included about 300 Spanish adventurers—at least three of whom were women. In addition, there were more than 1,000 Native Americans in the service of Coronado, as well as several Franciscan priests. About 1,500 horses and other pack animals carried the supplies needed for the huge expedition.

What happened to the Zunis?

When Coronado ordered the Zunis to surrender peacefully to him, they shot arrows and hurled stones at him and his party. But the Zunis were no match for the horses, lances, and guns of the Spanish conquistadors, and were quickly overpowered. The conquistadors took over the Zunis' settlement and stole their food, but to their disappointment found no gold or treasure.

Who were Lewis and Clark?

Meriwether Lewis was the man chosen by Thomas Jefferson, third President of the United States, to lead an important expedition. Once appointed, Lewis asked his friend William Clark to join him as co-leader. Together they headed a group of soldiers, explorers, and others who made up the Corps of Discovery. The task of the expedition was to travel through the territory that lay west of the Mississippi River and find out about the land, people, rivers, and anything else of interest in this vast, unknown region.

Who bought Louisiana?

In 1803, in one of the biggest bargains in history, Jefferson bought a vast area of land west of the Mississippi River and north of the Gulf of Mexico. The region was called Louisiana. Jefferson paid the French $15 million for it. The purchase more than doubled the size of the United States.

Where did the Corps set off from?

The Corps spent the winter in a camp just outside St Louis, where the Missouri and the Mississippi rivers meet. It set off on its famous journey on the afternoon of May 14, 1804.

Meriwether Lewis (left) and William Clark.

What did the expedition take to eat?

Not much. Lewis and Clark took with them only a few provisions intended for emergencies only. They planned to hunt and fish for food, and to barter with the Native Americans that they met on their travels.

Lewis and Clark took presents to give to the Native Americans that they met on their expedition.

How many people were there in the Corps?

When it set off, the Corps probably numbered about 40 to 50 people (the number is not known for certain). It included soldiers, several boatmen, a hunter named George Drouillard, and Clark's slave named York, as well as Lewis's large Newfoundland dog!

Why did Lewis and Clark make the incredible journey?

President Jefferson was delighted about the purchase of Louisiana; the problem was that he did not really know what he had bought. No one knew the exact size of Louisiana, and the only information about the land came from fur trappers. So Jefferson decided to send Lewis and Clark on their historic journey "to explore the Mississippi River...for the purposes of commerce."

Who took a medal of peace?

One of the aims of the expedition was to find out about the Native Americans living in the newly purchased Louisiana Territory. Lewis and Clark had strict instructions from President Jefferson to keep up good relations with the Native Americans that they met on the journey. They took with them many goods to offer as gifts, including beads, mirrors, combs, ribbons, cloth, knives, and fishhooks. They also carried a special peace medal, which showed hands clasped in friendship on one side and President Jefferson on the other.

How did the Corps travel?

The Corps of Discovery set off on its journey up the Missouri River. It traveled in a large boat, called a keelboat, which measured 55 ft (17 m) long and could float in very shallow water. The boat had a few cabins, but most of the crew lived and slept on deck under canvas covers. The keelboat could be sailed if the wind was in the right direction, or rowed or towed along by human power. The expedition also took with it two large canoes, called pirogues, which were each about 40 ft (12 m) long.

Who needed a collapsible boat?

Lewis took a collapsible boat for use later in the expedition. He knew that the keelboat and pirogues would be left behind at some point, so he carefully designed an iron framework, which was packed into crates. Unfortunately, when the boat was eventually put together, it did not float, and Lewis was forced to abandon it.

What helped the expedition?

In August 1805, the expedition entered territory under the control of the Shoshone tribe. At first the Shoshone were suspicious of the explorers. But just when things began to look threatening, Sacajawea recognized the Shoshone chief—it was her brother whom she had not seen since she was a child. There was great rejoicing as the two were reunited.

What animals did the expedition meet?

The members of the Corps of Discovery came across a bewildering array of wildlife during the expedition. They saw vast herds of antelope, buffalo, and elk, and described some frightening encounters with grizzly bears. They investigated the burrows of prairie dogs, watched Bighorn sheep walk across seemingly vertical cliff faces, and shot a Californian condor that had a wingspan of nearly 10 ft (3 m).

Who was Sacajawea?

The first winter of the expedition (1804–1805), the Corps built a fort near the villages of the Mandan tribe. During their stay at Fort Mandan, Lewis and Clark hired a French-Canadian trader named Toussaint Charbonneau and his wife Sacajawea. Their baby son, Jean Baptiste, also joined the expedition. Sacajawea was a Native American of the Shoshone tribe. She had been kidnapped as a child. As a result of her local knowledge and contacts, she quickly became a vital member of the Corps of Discovery.

Sacajawea, the expedition's Native American guide, points the way.

Lewis and Clark by the Columbia River.

How long were Lewis and Clark away?

The Corps of Discovery was away for nearly two and a half years, during which time it traveled an estimated 3,700 mi (5,950 km). The explorers sailed up the Missouri River, crossed the fearsome Rocky Mountains, and braved the rapids of the mighty Columbia River before reaching present-day Oregon and the Pacific Ocean. They spent the winter of 1805–1806 in Fort Clatsop on the Pacific coast. The outward journey took 18 months, but the journey home only six months! The Corps arrived back in St Louis on September 23, 1806, to the cheers of the townspeople.

Was the expedition a success?

The short answer is yes! The expedition returned safely, with the loss of only one member. Lewis and Clark made maps of the territory they crossed, and described hundreds of plants and animals previously unknown to Americans. And, as instructed by President Jefferson, the Corps struck up peaceful relations with the Native Americans that they met on their journey.

How did the expedition celebrate Christmas?

Christmas 1805 was spent in the confined quarters of Fort Clatsop. The explorers gave each other small gifts such as wool clothing, a Native American basket, silk handkerchiefs, and moccasins. They celebrated with singing and dancing, and a week later greeted the New Year with a salute fired from their rifles into the air.

Who shot Meriwether Lewis?

One day, while out hunting, a short-sighted member of the expedition saw a movement in the grass and shot at what he thought was an elk. Unfortunately it turned out to be his commanding officer, Meriwether Lewis. Luckily the wound was not life-threatening, and it healed rapidly over the next few weeks.

What does Nez Perce mean?

Nez Perce was the name given by French traders to a Native American tribe that lived in the Rocky Mountains. It means "pierced nose," and was given because the members of the tribe wore ornaments through their noses. Nez Perce guides gave vital help to the Corps as it crossed the mountains.

What happened at the Short and Long Narrows?

In October 1805, the expedition reached the mighty Columbia River. By this time the Corps was traveling in five dugout canoes. When the water became too rough for the canoes, the explorers had to pull them out and carry them and all their equipment to a calmer part of the river. But when they reached the Short and Long Narrows—a terrifying stretch of rapids between towering cliffs—there was little choice but to continue through the turbulant waters. Despite their unwieldy canoes, the brave explorers survived, to the astonishment of the local Native Americans.

Who followed Brigham Young?

The second leader of the Mormons—after the death of Joseph Smith—was Brigham Young. He knew that Smith had made plans to move his people to the wide open spaces of the Great Basin beneath the Rocky Mountains. Young decided to put this plan into action. When the Mormons were hounded out of Nauvoo in 1846, he led about 12,000 people along the Mormon Trail, across the Mississippi River, through Iowa and Nebraska, and across the Rockies.

Who said: "This is the place"?

In July 1847, a small party of Mormons led by Brigham Young stopped on an arid, treeless plateau. Looking around him, Young said: "This is the right place." This was the Great Salt Lake valley, and it was here that the Mormons founded Salt Lake City, in present-day Utah.

Mormons on their long journey to Utah. They were led by Brigham Young.

What happened on June 27, 1844?

On June 27, 1844, in the town of Nauvoo, Illinois, an angry mob broke into the local jail, dragged out a man named Joseph Smith, and shot him dead. Smith was the founder and leader of the Church of Jesus Christ of Latter Day Saints—the Mormons. Smith and his followers had been persecuted ever since the founding of the Mormon Church in 1830. The Mormons had already been forced to move from New York State first to Ohio, then to Missouri and Illinois, where Smith was murdered.

Why was Joseph Smith murdered?

One of the beliefs of the Mormon religion was that a man could marry more than one wife—a practice known as polygamy. It upset people wherever the Mormons went, and led to Smith's murder in Nauvoo, Illinois.

Who was killed in the Mountain Meadows Massacre of 1857?

In 1857, the Mormons were on the lookout for hostile government troops. In September, a wagon train passed through Mormon territory and, convinced that it was a threat, the Mormons attacked, helped by some Paiuté Native Americans. In fact, the wagon train was full of pioneers, more than 100 of whom were killed.

How did the Mormons survive?

When the Mormons arrived in the inhospitable region chosen to be their home, they had to work extremely hard to survive. Under Young's leadership, they dug irrigation channels and used water from the surrounding hills to water their crops. Fifty years later, much of the barren desert had been transformed into a fruitful land.

Where was Deseret?

The Kingdom of Deseret—meaning "Land of the Honey Bee"—was the name that the Mormons gave to their new homeland. Young wanted to extend Deseret westward to the Pacific Ocean, but the government had other ideas. Instead, the Utah Territory was created in 1850, with reduced boundaries.

A Mormon pioneer family outside their cabin in Echo City, Utah, in 1869.

What was a "prairie schooner"?

More than 1,000 people set off along the Oregon Trail in 1843, the start of the "Great Migration" to the West. They traveled in heavy wooden wagons called Conestoga wagons, pulled by horses, mules, or oxen. Later pioneers along the trail used lighter wagons. These were known as "prairie schooners," because their white canvas tops resembled the sails of a kind of ship called a schooner. The settlers packed the wagons with their belongings and with supplies for the journey. Only babies and sick people rode in the wagons—everyone else walked.

What did the men do?

The men in a wagon train were responsible for driving and repairing the wagons and looking after the livestock. They also hunted for food and took turns standing guard at night, keeping watch for hostile Native Americans.

How long was the journey?

The journey from Missouri to Oregon took about five months. The pioneers usually set off in April, because it was vital for them to cross the coastal mountains (the Cascades and the Sierra Nevada) before the winter snows set in. If they left too early, they ran the risk that there would not be enough grass for their livestock.

Where did the Oregon and California trails go?

In 1840, fewer than 150 Americans lived in the vast area of the West known as Oregon. Only five years later, thousands of people had settled there. Most had traveled across the continent along the 2,000-mile (3,200-km) Oregon Trail. This trail usually started in Independence, Missouri, crossed the Great Plains and the Rocky Mountains, and ended in the Columbia River region. An alternative trail, the California Trail, followed the same route until Fort Hall, west of the Rocky Mountains, where it branched southward, ending in the Sacramento valley.

The Oregon Trail and the California Trail both began in Independence, Missouri.

Fort Vancouver

Fort Hall

San Francisco

Fort Bridger

Independence

Oregon Trail

California Trail

What were the women's jobs?

During the long, arduous journey, the women on a wagon train were in charge of preparing food. They got up before dawn to light fires and get the food ready. They also washed and mended clothes, and looked after the children and anyone who was sick.

Why did so many pioneers die?

Thousands of people died along the Oregon and California trails. One estimate is that seven people died for every mile of the route. The biggest killer was disease, particularly cholera. However, the greatest fear for the pioneers was attack from Native Americans. In fact, very few people died as a result of such attacks.

Cooking over a camp fire.

How many wagons were there in a wagon train?

Settlers traveled in groups along the trail for safety and for companionship, and there could be anything up to 100 wagons in a wagon train. The train traveled very slowly—at little over 1 mph (1.5 kph) and was on the move for nine or 10 hours every day.

Who was in charge of the train?

In the spring, groups of pioneers met in rendezvous towns such as Independence or St Joseph, Missouri, or Council Bluffs, Iowa. They formed wagon-train companies and elected a leader, known as the raid captain. They also employed guides to lead them along the trail.

What happened at night?

At the end of a long day on the trail, the wagons would draw up into circles and set up camp for the night. These wagon circles gave the settlers protection in case of attack from Native Americans.

A pioneer wagon loaded with a family's possessions.

Who wore bloomers?

Many pioneer women found that the heavy, full-length dresses that were the usual dress of the period were hopelessly impractical for life on the trail. Some women started to wear shorter dresses that did not reach all the way to the ground; others even dared to wear "bloomers"—a type of pants.

What was life like on a trail drive?

Trail drives lasted three or four months. At first the cowboys had to live on what they could carry and cook for themselves. They ate mostly beans and hard bread. Later, when trail drives became more organized, a chuck wagon accompanied the cowboys carrying food, water, and other supplies.

What was a cattle drive?

Trail drives started in the south, in Texas, near the Gulf of Mexico. Two or three thousand cattle were rounded up and then driven day after day, week after week, northward to the nearest railroad junction. The first of these railroad links was Abilene in Kansas. The trail drive from Texas to Abilene took about three months and became known as the Chisholm Trail. The earliest trail drives were in 1867, when an estimated 35,000 cattle made the journey along the Chisholm Trail.

What was a bronco?

One of a cowboy's jobs on the ranch was to break in untamed horses, called broncos. First he would single out a wild horse and catch it with a lassoo. Then he had to blindfold and saddle the horse and mount it. The horse, which had never been ridden before, would buck and rear, and try to throw the cowboy from its back. Many cowboys were injured trying to tame broncos.

Why did the cattle move so slowly?

On the trail, it was important not to drive the cattle too hard. They needed to arrive at the railhead in good condition. On the journey, the cattle grazed on the grass that was freely available across the Great Plains. As well as the Chisholm Trail, there were other trails including the Shawnee, the Western, and the Goodnight-Loving Trail.

A trail drive boss in Montana, 1888.

What was a ranch?

As the cattle business boomed, some Texas cattlemen set up large farms, known as ranches. The ranch owner employed cowboys to work full-time looking after his cattle. The owner lived in a house in the center of the ranch; the cowboys often lived in bunkhouses.

How did the secret get out?

Marshall and Sutter tried to keep their discovery a secret. But, while Sutter tried unsuccessfully to claim the land on which the sawmill stood, rumor started to spread. At first, workers at the sawmill did some quiet prospecting, then their neighbors joined in and the news began to spread.

John Sutter. The California Gold Rush began when gold was found by one of his workers.

Who found gold in California?

On a January morning in 1848, a carpenter named James Marshall was sent by his employer, John Sutter, to inspect some work on a sawmill. The mill was on a bend of the American River in California. As Marshall inspected a ditch dug out of the bed of the millstream, he noticed something glittering on the bottom. He bent down and saw several golden-yellow rocks, about the size of small peas. Marshall had found gold!

What did the diary say?

An entry in the diary of one of the workmen working at Sutter's Mill agrees with Marshall's story of the discovery of the gold. It reads: "This day some kind of mettle [metal] was found in the tail race that looks like goald [gold]. First discovered by James Martial [Marshall], the Boss of the Mill."

How old were cowboys?

The average age of a cowboy was 24. Many cowboys were Mexicans and some were African-Americans. Most earned no more than $30 a month. Their lives were incredibly tough. They owned their clothes, precious saddles, and guns, but little else. Only a few owned their own horses.

Who was Joseph G. McCoy?

It is claimed that McCoy was the first person to organize a trail drive. He recruited experienced cowboys from Texas to drive the herds northward. In Texas the cattle would fetch no more than $4 a head: in Kansas the price was nearer $40!

What did President Polk show to Congress?

At first, not everyone believed in the wild tales of gold coming from the West. Many people back East dismissed the tales as rumors. But in December 1848, President Polk showed a tea box full of gold dust to Congress—proof that the rumors were true!

Who were the "forty-niners"?

Once President Polk had proved that there really was a goldmine in the American West, the "Gold Rush" began. In 1849, about 80,000 people from all over the globe arrived in California. They became known as the "forty-niners."

Who wrote: "Go West, young man, go West!"?

These words appeared in an American newspaper editorial in 1851. By that time, many thousands of hopeful gold-seekers had already headed West across the American continent in the hope of making their fortunes. Most of them were men who left behind homes and families, intending to return after a few months or years, rich beyond their wildest dreams. Very few succeeded.

Where were Lousy Ravine and Bogus Thunder?

These are both names of gold-mining camps in California, long since abandoned. Names of gold camps and towns often told their own stories, such as You Bet, Git-Up-and-Git, and Bedbug!

What are ghost towns?

Today, you can see many reminders of the Gold Rush in the American West. The gold miners built camps and towns wherever they struck gold, and abandoned them just as quickly when the gold ran out. Many of these towns survive as "ghost towns"— empty and in ruins.

These prospectors are using a "long tom" to search for gold. The running water separated out pieces of gold from dirt, stones, and other waste.

An early advertisement for Levi jeans.

What did Levi Strauss sell to the prospectors?

Levi Strauss was a German immigrant living in New York when the Gold Rush started. He traveled to the West and sold cotton material, which he advertised as being ideal for making tents. However, it turned out to be more suitable for pants—the first Levis.

What did a shout of: "Color!" mean?

It meant that the prospectors had struck lucky and found gold. The early prospectors discovered gold quite easily on the beds of rivers and streams. They used a flat "pan" to swirl a mixture of gravel and water around until the lighter gravel was washed away, leaving the heavier gold behind. As time went on, finding gold became harder. Prospectors had to dig deeper and use long wooden boxes called cradles to sort the mud and gravel from any gold.

How did the gold seekers get to California?

There were many different routes to reach the goldfields—all dangerous. Many people walked overland, some as far as 2,000 miles (3,200 km). Others went by sea to Panama, traveled overland to the Pacific Ocean, and continued to San Francisco by sea. Many died before they reached California.

Where did barkeepers find gold?

On the floor of the bar! Many miners used pinches of gold dust to pay for refreshment. After a long night of serving drinks, barkeepers in California would pan the floor of the saloon to pick up any gold that had fallen there!

How much did an egg cost?

When they arrived in California, prospectors were amazed at the cost of accommodation, tools such as picks and shovels, and food. One egg cost as much as $3. The gold-seekers had little choice but to pay up.

A poster advertising voyages from New York to San Francisco in California. Sailing was the quickest way to get there—and the most expensive.

Merchants' Express Line of Clipper Ships
FOR
SAN FRANCISCO!
NONE BUT A 1 FAST SAILING CLIPPERS LOADED IN THIS LINE.

THE EXTREME CLIPPER SHIP
OCEAN EXPRESS
WATSON, COMMANDER,
AT PIER 9, EAST RIVER.
This splendid vessel is one of the fastest Clippers afloat, and a great favorite with
shippers. Her commander, Capt. WATSON, was formerly master of the celebra
Clipper "FLYING DRAGON," which made the passage in 97 days, an
the ship POLYNESIA, which made the passage in 103 days.
She comes to the berth one third loaded, and has very large engagements.
RANDOLPH M. COOLEY,
WATER ST., cor. Wall, Tontine Buil

Who built the railroad across America?

In 1862, Congress passed an Act to authorize the construction of a railroad that would link the east and the west coasts of America. Two companies were given contracts to build the railroad. The Union Pacific started in Omaha, Nebraska, and worked westward. The Central Pacific started in Sacramento, west of the Sierra Nevada mountains, and worked eastward. Construction of the tracks started in 1863 and took over five years to complete.

Who worked for the Central Pacific?

Not only did the Central Pacific company have to bring its supplies by ship around South America, it also had to drive the railroad through the Sierra Nevada mountains. To do this work, thousands of laborers were recruited in China and brought to California.

Who won the railroad race?

The Union Pacific company laid more track than the Central Pacific company. Building the eastern part of the railroad across the Great Plains, it had the advantage of a direct supply route from the east.

Why was it a race?

The government paid the two companies between $16,000 and $48,000 per mile of track laid, depending on the difficulty of the terrain. The companies also received land on either side of the track. Not surprisingly, construction turned into a race between the two companies to see which could lay the most track.

The railroad linked the east and west coasts of the United States.

What happened when the companies met?

Workers from the two companies building the railroad came face to face in Utah. At first they kept building, refusing to stop because they were paid for every mile of track laid. The government stepped in to order the line to meet at Promontory Summit, but not before a few fights had broken out between workers from the rival companies.

What did the Native Americans think of the railroad?

The railroad cut through Native American land. White hunters shot thousands of buffalo to feed the hungry railroad workers. The Native Americans showed their anger by attacking the construction crews.

How many Chinese laborers died for the railroad?

It is estimated that more than 1,000 Chinese workers died during the construction of the railroad. In the Sierra Nevada mountains, they had to blast holes with dynamite into solid rock, working in baskets precariously slung by ropes over huge drops.

How was the track laid?

Every part of the track was laid by hand. Advance parties leveled out the land ready for the heavy crossways timbers, called ties. The iron rails were laid on to the timbers and attached with spikes and bolts. Only two or three miles of track were laid each day.

What happened on May 10, 1869?

In May 1869, at Promontory Summit, Utah, the tracks of the Union Pacific and the Central Pacific companies finally met. The governor of California and president of the Central Pacific, Leland Stanford, lifted the hammer and brought it down to hit the last spike in the track—a golden one. He missed the first time. The telegraph man sent the news: "DONE!" In Washington D.C. a great cheer greeted the news, and in San Francisco celebrations began.

Hammering in a golden spike at the point where the Union Pacific and Central Pacific railroads met.

Who first robbed trains?

In October 1866, members of the Reno Gang held up a train on the Ohio and Mississippi Railroad, stealing more than $13,000. The Reno gang was just one of the many gangs of outlaws that terrorised the West during the pioneer years, robbing banks, stagecoaches, and trains, and stealing horses and cattle.

Who was Billy the Kid?

A notorious outlaw, Billy the Kid was said to have killed 27 people before his early death at the age of 21. It is hard to know who he was—in his early years he went by the name of Henry McCarty. Later he called himself William H. Bonney Jr.

What happened in Northfield, Minnesota, in 1876?

On September 7, 1876, the infamous James-Younger Gang, led by brothers Jesse and Frank James, held up the First National Bank of Northfield. The cashier refused to open the vault, and the townspeople shot at the bank robbers. Most of the gang were killed or captured. Only the James brothers escaped.

Was Jesse James a hero?

Many myths and romantic stories grew up about the outlaws of the Wild West. The bandit Jesse James was often portrayed as a Robin Hood figure who stole from the rich to help the poor. In fact, he was a callous and brutal thief who thought nothing of attacking and killing unarmed and defenseless people.

The infamous Jesse James posed for this photograph in 1864, during the American Civil War.

How did bandits hold up a train?

Bandits in the Wild West would often strike at night, signaling with a red lantern to stop a train. They would then board the train and use dynamite to blow open the safe where the money was stored. Banknotes were sometimes blown far and wide, and the bandits had to collect them up quickly before disappearing into the night.

The Reno Gang prepare to rob a train on the move.

What were "Pinkerton men"?

Allan Pinkerton (1819–1884) set up one of the first detective agencies in the United States. His employees, known as "Pinkerton men," were responsible for capturing many outlaws, including the infamous Reno Gang.

Why was Belle Starr called the "Bandit Queen"?

Women, as well as men, turned to violence as a way of life in the Wild West. One of the most famous female bandits was Belle Starr. Her skill on horseback, armed with a brace of pistols, earned her the title "Bandit Queen."

This Colt revolver was owned by the outlaw Jesse James.

What was the Hole in the Wall?

The Hole in the Wall was the name of a gorge that was home to 30–40 or more bandits in the 1890s. It lay about 50 miles (80 km) south of Buffalo, in Wyoming. Most of the outlaws were cattle or horse thieves. They were known as the "Wild Bunch," and the most famous members were Butch Cassidy and the Sundance Kid.

What happened at the O.K. Corral?

In 1881, a gunfight broke out between rival gangs at the O.K. Corral in Tombstone, Arizona. Involved in the fight was Wyatt Earp. Although a lawman—he served as a deputy sheriff and a marshal—he had a history as violent and colorful as that of many criminals.

What happened to the buffalo?

The Native American tribes of the Great Plains had long relied on the buffalo for their livelihoods. Then came the building of the railroad across the Plains, and with it a massive increase in buffalo-hunting by white Americans. The Native Americans were unable to prevent buffalo-hunters coming in their thousands to shoot the seemingly limitless herds. In the south, over four million buffalo were shot between 1872 and 1874. In the north, the buffalo herd was destroyed in the early 1880s.

Who wanted the buffalo destroyed?

Some Americans thought that killing off the buffalo would force Native Americans into submission. Without the buffalo, they would have to rely on farming and government hand-outs for food. Other people were horrified and tried to stop the slaughter, but they failed.

What was buffalo hide used for?

In the 1870s there was a huge demand for buffalo hides. The hides were made into leather for shoes and other products. They were also used to make belts to drive the machinery in factories.

Millions of buffalo were killed by professional hunters in the early 1870s.

The Sioux Reservation at Pine Ridge, South Dakota, in 1890.

Who died at the Battle of Little Bighorn?

In June 1876, General George A. Custer led a group of soldiers to drive the defiant Sioux off their land in the Black Hills and on to a reservation. Custer found the Native Americans' camp at Little Bighorn on June 25 and decided to attack immediately. What he did not know was that at least 2,000 Native American warriors were in the camp, together with their leaders Sitting Bull and Chief Crazy Horse. Custer and his men were defeated and killed by the Native Americans, sending shock waves through white American society.

What were Native American reservations?

As more settlers moved into the West, they often came into conflict with the native peoples who had been living in the region for many generations. In the 1850s and 1860s, the government made various treaties with the peoples of the Great Plains, establishing peaceful relations and promising them specific areas of land, known as reservations. Despite the treaties, there were many battles between the U.S. army and Native American warriors, who did not want to move on to the reservations.

What was the worst tragedy for the Sioux?

In one violent episode, more than 150 Native Americans, including women and children, were massacred by the army at Wounded Knee, South Dakota. About 30 soldiers also died. After the massacre, the remaining Sioux had little choice but to move to the reservation set aside for them by the government.

Where did the Nez Perce go?

Whole tribes were forced to move thousands of miles away to live on new reservations. The Nez Perce lived in the northwest, in Oregon. They tried to live peacefully with the settlers, but eventually violence erupted. Despite fighting hard to keep their land, they were eventually forced to move to a reservation in Oklahoma.

What happened when gold was discovered in the Black Hills?

In 1874, gold was discovered in the Black Hills of South Dakota. The gold was on territory controlled by the Sioux. Soon miners were flooding into the Black Hills, ignoring the Native Americans' rights over the land. Violence erupted, and the Sioux were ordered by the government to leave, but they refused to go.

Who danced the Ghost Dance?

In the desperate times of the late 1800s, many Native Americans in the West turned in hope to a new movement known as the Ghost Dance. The Ghost Dance helped Native Americans to cope with the destruction of the buffalo and the loss of their lands by promising a return to the old ways of life and better times.

The Civil War

Union soldier

Who were the two sides in the Civil War?

American fought against American. On one side were the forces of the North, or Union. They represented the 23 Northern states of the elected government. On the other side were the forces of the South, or Confederacy, who fought for the 11 Southern states. These rebel states had broken away from the Union and elected their own president.

When did the Civil War take place?

Confederate forces first opened fire at Fort Sumter, Charleston, on April 12, 1861. Four years later, almost exactly, the main Confederate forces under General Robert E. Lee surrendered at Appomattox on April 9, 1865. The last Confederates to surrender did so on May 26.

Which states were in the Confederacy?

Alabama, Arkansas, Florida, Georgia, Louisiana, Mississippi, North and South Carolina, Tennessee, Texas, and Virginia. There were also some "border states." Rebel governments in Kentucky and Missouri supported the South.

Which state had two presidents?

Kentucky. The President of the Union, Abraham Lincoln, and the President of the Confederacy, Jefferson Davis, were both born in Kentucky, near the Ohio River.

Abraham Lincoln

Which side had the most money?

In the North were located America's big cities, industries, commerce, factories, and railroads. It boasted 75 percent of the nation's wealth. The South was much poorer, and derived much of its wealth from cotton, grown on plantations worked by slaves.

Confederate soldier

What kind of war was it?

The Civil War is often described as the first "modern" war. Many modern weapons were first used in this conflict, yet the tactics were very old-fashioned. The combined result created high numbers of casualties.

How many people supported the opposing sides?

The South had a population of about 9 million people. Of these, more than 3 million were black slaves. The North found volunteers for its army in a much larger population of more than 21 million.

Which states were in the Union?

California, Connecticut, Delaware, Illinois, Indiana, Iowa, Kansas, Kentucky, Maine, Maryland, Massachusetts, Michigan, Minnesota, Missouri, New Hampshire, New Jersey, New York, Ohio, Oregon, Pennsylvania, Rhode Island, Vermont, and Wisconsin. In addition, the "organized territories" of Colorado, Dakota, Nebraska, Nevada, New Mexico, Utah, and Washington wished to join the Union as free states.

What did Walt Whitman say about the Civil War?

The famous poet called it that "strange, sad war." His phrase described the nature of the war perfectly. It was a war in which brother fought against brother, and a nation slaughtered its own finest men. Whitman witnessed the conflict firsthand as a volunteer in a military hospital. He wrote: "Future years will never know the seething hell and black infernal background... and it is best they should not."

Where did the fighting take place?

The war took place in two main regions, divided by the Appalachian Mountains. East to the Atlantic, most battles took place in Virginia between the two capitals, Washington and Richmond. To the west, the two sides fought for control of the Mississippi River. The North also blockaded the South's coast with ships in the Atlantic and Gulf of Mexico.

Who were the "Border Ruffians"?

In 1854, it was decided that the inhabitants of the new territory of Kansas could vote on being a slave state or a free state. Pro-slavery gangs, called "Border Ruffians," rushed from Missouri to Kansas to cast illegal votes and to attack abolitionist voters.

What was the Missouri Compromise of 1820?

In 1819, there were 11 "slave" and 11 "free" states. To preserve this balance, when the slave state of Missouri joined the Union in 1820, Maine joined as a free state. The government agreed that no new slave states north of Missouri would be admitted to the Union. For the first time, the Union had been divided into North and South.

How many black slaves were there?

There were over 3 million black slaves on the cotton plantations of the South. Slaves were recognized as property in the U.S. Constitution.

Border Ruffians wanted to force people to vote to keep slavery in Kansas.

Who lived in Uncle Tom's Cabin?

A character in the novel of that name. The book was written in 1852 by Harriet Beecher Stowe. Her sentimental story described the evils of slavery, which was an accepted practice in the South. It sold 300,000 copies in its first year. The novel, and plays based on it, persuaded many people in the North to become "abolitionists"— people who wished to ban slavery. Many Southerners were outraged by it, and saw it as an attack on their way of life.

Who was "Moses"?

This was the name slaves gave to Harriet Tubman. After escaping slavery in 1849, she returned south 19 times to lead over 300 slaves to freedom. She was part of the "Underground Railroad," the secret organization that led slaves to freedom in the North.

Why was Abraham Lincoln elected President in 1860?

Lincoln's Republican Party, formed in 1854, was elected because the vote for the Democratic Party was split between two candidates. Lincoln became President without winning a single Southern state, many of whom refused to put his name on the poll.

John Brown was the leader of the abolitionists.

What was the Fugitive Slave Law?

It was a law passed as part of a new "compromise" in 1850. To keep the South happy, the law made it possible to return slaves who had escaped to the North to their owners. It created fury in the North. Poet Ralph Waldo Emerson called it a "filthy law."

Why do people sing about John Brown?

On October 16, 1859, fanatical abolitionist John Brown led a raid on the armory at Harper's Ferry, Virginia. He planned to steal enough weapons to lead a slave uprising in Virginia. His plan was foiled by U.S. Marines, and Brown was hanged in December. The soldiers of the North remembered Brown when they marched to war singing: "John Brown's body lies a'moldering in the grave."

Which state was the first to leave the Union?

South Carolina, which declared the Union "dissolved" on December 20, 1860. The other slave states soon followed, and on February 8, 1861, they declared a new nation—the Confederate States of America.

Where was the capital of the Union?

Stars and Stripes

It remained in Washington D.C. From the White House window, Lincoln could watch Confederate forces gathering. Until May 1861, when 10,000 Union troops arrived, there was a danger that Washington would be captured.

What flag did the North fight under?

The Stars and Stripes. War broke out when the South bombarded Fort Sumter, South Carolina, which was still under federal jurisdiction and flying the American flag. After surrendering, the fort commander took the tattered flag away with him. He returned to rehoist the same flag four years later.

The White House was the capital of the Union.

Who was Abraham Lincoln?

Lincoln was President and commander-in-chief of the North's forces. He was a striking figure at 6 ft 4 in (1.9 m) tall, and a brilliant speaker. Lincoln had little military experience, but turned out to be a good commander. On March 4, 1861, he traveled to his inauguration in secret because of an assassination plot. In his speech he said: "In your hands, my dissatisfied fellow countrymen, and not in mine, is the momentous issue of civil war."

General McClellan

What may a black sentry have told Ulysses S. Grant?

On seeing an officer walk past smoking, the sentry is famously supposed to have said: "You must throw away that cigar, sir!"

Who were the Graybeards?

The Graybeards were a regiment of men all aged 45 or more. Other regiments fighting for the North were also given nicknames: Perry's Saints (all officers were ministers); La Garde Lafayette (French New Yorkers); Teacher's Regiment (mainly college professors).

Who was George B. McClellan?

McClellan was the cautious commander of the North's troops in the early part of the war. When he complained about fatigued horses, Lincoln wrote: "Will you pardon me for asking what the horses of your army have done ... to fatigue anything?"

Which songs did the North sing?

Their songs included *Yankee Doodle, We'll Rally Round the Flag,* and *The Girl I Left Behind Me. The Battle Hymn of the Republic* and *John Brown's Body* were sung to a tune that came from the South.

Who was General Ulysses S. Grant?

Grant was the victorious commander of the North's troops at the end of the war. He had become a hero in 1862 when he demanded unconditional surrender from a Confederate general. Supporters said his initials stood for "Unconditional Surrender," and sent him so many cigars that he gave up his pipe. When prohibitionists complained that Grant drank heavily, Lincoln replied: "What brand does he drink? I'd like to send a barrel of it to the other generals."

What names were given to the Union forces?

They were known as the Union, the Federal Army, the Republic, the North, the Yanks or Yankees, and the Blues. Confederate soldiers nicknamed the Union soldiers "Billy Yank."

Who was Robert E. Lee?

L ee was the greatest soldier of the Civil War. He commanded the Marines who arrested John Brown at Harper's Ferry. When the war broke out, he was offered command of the North's forces, but declined through loyalty to his home state of Virginia. He took command of the South's forces in 1862 and proved himself to be a daring and brilliant commander. His soldiers were devoted to him and named him "Marse Lee."

Where was the capital of the Confederacy?

The Confederacy's capital was Richmond, just 103 miles (166 km) south of Washington. When the North learned that the Confederate Congress was to meet there in July 1861, the New York Tribune started a famous warcry: "Forward to Richmond! Forward to Richmond!"

Stars and Bars

Why did the South have two flags?

The official Confederate flag, the Stars and Bars, was very similar to the Stars and Stripes of the North. So, a red "battle flag" with stars on a blue saltire (diagonal cross) was also used. The first of these flags were made from silk intended for ladies' dresses.

What names were given to the Confederate forces?

They were known as the Confederates, the South, the Rebels, and the Grays. Union soldiers nicknamed their Confederate enemy "Johnny Reb."

The ruins of the arsenal at Richmond

Battle flag

What songs did the Confederates sing?

The songs of the South included *The Yellow Rose of Texas* and *The Bonnie Blue Flag*. The most famous song of the South, *Dixie*, was actually written in the North by the son of an abolitionist.

Robert E. Lee

How many horses were shot from under Nathan Bedford Forrest?

Forrest was a brilliant cavalry commander for the South. He started the war as a private and progressed to major general. Forrest had 29 horses shot from under him during the war, and was frequently injured. Sherman called him "the very Devil."

How big was the South's army?

At the start of the war, the Confederates created a regular army of 10,000 soldiers. The tradition, though, was for civilian volunteers to fight. In all, some one million men fought for the South during the Civil War.

Was Robert E. Lee born to be a soldier?

Yes. Lee came from a famous military family. His father, Henry "Light Horse Harry" Lee, was George Washington's favorite cavalry commander. He also had ancestors who had fought with William the Conqueror and in the Crusades.

Who was Jefferson Davis?

Davis took the oath as President of the Confederacy on February 18, 1861. A graduate of West Point, he would have preferred a commission in the army. Just as Lee was not a supporter of slavery, so Davis was famous for his kindness to his slaves. He was imprisoned for two years after the war for treason. Seven Southern states still celebrate a legal holiday on his birthday, June 3.

Who were the Yankee Hunters?

The Barbour County Yankee Hunters was the nickname of one of the Confederates' units. Others were the Cherokee Lincoln Killers, the Hornet's Nest Riflemen, and the Tallapossa Thrashers.

Did any women sign up to fight?

As many as 400 women disguised themselves as men so that they could enlist. They were able to do this because the doctors who examined new recruits barely looked at them. One famous soldier was Jennie Hodgers, an Irishwoman who joined the 95th Illinois Volunteers under the name of Albert Cashier. Her sex remained undiscovered throughout the war, and she fought in several major battles and received a pension after the armistice.

How did firearms develop during the Civil War?

Before the war, soldiers fired round balls from flintlock muskets with smooth barrels. These were difficult to load and usually missed their target. General Grant said the enemy could "fire at you all day without your finding it out." The muskets were quickly replaced by rifles with grooves cut into the barrels, which fired pointed bullets. These were easier to load, more powerful, and deadly accurate. Both sides now had the firepower to inflict terrible casualties.

Women were able to join the army by pretending to be men.

Union soldiers setting up a cannon

Did all the soldiers use the same weapons?

No, volunteers arrived with all kinds of weapons. In addition, both governments bought poor firearms from abroad. These were known as "pumpkin slingers" because they were so heavy and clumsy, and "mules" because they had a terrible "kick," or recoil.

Could people avoid conscription?

Rich people on both sides could pay for a "substitute" to fight in their place. This might cost a Southern farmer up to $6,000. The arrival of unfit substitutes horrified professional soldiers. One substitute was said to have been lured from an asylum.

How was the war similar to World War I?

As the war dragged on, regiments defended their positions by digging trenches and protecting them with wire entanglements, tripwires, earthworks, and sharpened stakes. They invented many of the tactics and defenses used in World War I.

Why did soldiers use bayonets as candlesticks?

Of all the wounds suffered in the Civil War, 94 percent were caused by bullets. Soldiers threw their bayonets away as useless, or drove them into the walls of their huts and used them as candlesticks.

Did families always fight on the same side?

No, the tragedy of the war was that it tore families apart. William and James Terrill were brothers who fought on opposite sides. Both rose to the rank of brigadier general and both were killed. President Lincoln's wife Mary had three half brothers who died fighting for the South.

What other inventions were used in the fighting during the Civil War?

A primitive flame-thrower was used by one General Butler, and camouflage must have been used, as Confederate troops wrote about shooting down "moving bushes."

Were there age limits for enlisting?

No, soldiers enlisted at all ages. Curtis King enlisted in Iowa's "Graybeards" regiment at the ripe old age of 80. The most famous youngster in the war was Johnny Clem, the "Drummer Boy of Chickamauga." He enlisted aged ten. At Chickamauga he used a sawn-off musket to shoot a Confederate officer who had shouted at him: "Stop you little Yankee devil!" When he retired in 1915 as Major General Clem, he was the last active soldier left from the war.

Who blew up the bridges?

In revenge for the many attacks on his transportation system, Brigadier General Herman Haupt wrote an instruction manual showing Union troops how to destroy Confederate railroads. He also invented the tools for the job: a rail-bending "hook" and a "torpedo" for blowing up bridges.

Who built rubber boats for spies?

Haupt was the North's transportation chief. His engineering genius masterminded the Union's excellent railroad system. He also built fortified and portable bridges, and portable rubber boats for spies. When Confederates sabotaged the North's railroads, Haupt's Construction Corps repaired them with incredible speed.

Who traveled by rail?

The North, which had a more advanced rail system, was able to transport its troops, heavy guns, and supplies from east to west much more quickly than the South. For many soldiers, the journey to the front was their first experience of a train journey.

Who was Allan Pinkerton?

Pinkerton had famously set up one of the first private detective agencies in 1850. After the war started, he escorted Lincoln to his inauguration and started a "secret service" for the Union.

The railroad was very new to the United States during the Civil War.

What brought the war to the people back home?

For the first time, photographers stumbled on to battlegrounds with their heavy equipment and asked soldiers to remain still while they took their photos. The most famous photographer was New York's Mathew B. Brady. He shocked New York City in 1862 with an exhibition of photos of the dead. One visitor noted: "If he has not brought bodies and laid them in our dooryards, he has done something very like it."

A group of war correspondents from the New York Herald

New York Herald correspondents sketched and wrote notes on what they saw on the battlefield.

Which side had the best horses?

At the beginning of the war, troops from the rural South had the better cavalry. They were allowed to ride their own thoroughbreds, and came from a tradition of excellent cavalrymen.

Who invented a horseshoe machine?

The Union had much better technology. They invented a horseshoe machine that could produce 60 horseshoes a minute. As the South's mounts and equipment became exhausted, the North's improved.

Who were the spies?

Spies operated on both sides. The Union had a famous secret agent named Timothy Webster, who was hanged in 1862 for spying. The Confederates had a famous woman spy named Belle Boyd, who was known as the Siren of the Shenandoah.

What went up in the air to spy on the enemy?

Hot air balloons were used to spy on enemy positions. They were pioneered by showman Thaddeus Lowe, who founded the U.S. Balloon Corps after demonstrating a balloon to the president. From 300 ft (92 m), the pilot could help his gunners to aim, or relay details of enemy troop positions by telegraph. One balloon flew from the barge called the *George Washington Parke Custis*, making the barge the world's first aircraft carrier!

Who communicated using telescopes, flashlights, and telegraph?

Albert J. Myer founded the U.S. Army Signal Corps. He trained units of men to use telescopes, flags, flashlights, and the recent invention of the telegraph to set up a communications network for the North. By the end of the war, the many divisions of the vast army were linked by thousands of miles of telegraph wire.

What were "ironclads"?

The "ironclads" were a new type of ship that looked more like submarines. They had steam-driven propellers and were covered in armor plating. The South's *Merrimack* was an old frigate covered with flattened railroad tracks. Renamed *Virginia*, she sunk three of the North's ships on March 8, 1862. The following day she battled with the North's own ironclad, the *Monitor*, in the first sea battle between these strange craft. At this point in history, traditional wooden warships began to be replaced by modern battleships.

When did a submarine first sink a ship?

On February 17, 1864, the Confederate submarine *Hunley* attacked the Union ship *Housatonic*. The submarine was powered by eight infantrymen operating hand cranks. Its financial backer, Horace L. Hunley, had been killed during trial runs of this dangerous device, along with several crew members. The *Hunley* attacked with a "torpedo," which was actually a mine attached to a spear on the submarine's nose. The explosion sunk the ship, and also the submarine.

The St. Louis was the first ironclad gunboat built in the United States.

The early submarines were very dangerous vessels. Many men were killed in them.

Who flushed a toilet underwater?

The eccentric but brilliant Swedish engineer John Ericsson designed the first ironclads used by the North. He also invented the screw propeller, revolving gun turrets, an anchor with four flukes (the arrows that stick in the sea-bed), and a flush toilet that worked below the waterline.

How did Britain pay for the war?

The Geneva Tribunal of Arbitration decided in 1872 that Britain had not remained neutral because it had helped build Confederate ships. It had to pay the United States $15.5 million for the damage these ships did to the Union navy.

Who painted the Civil War in the English Channel?

The great French painter Manet depicted the sinking of the Confederate raider *Alabama* by the North's *Kearsarge* in the English Channel. Under the command of Captain Raphael Semmes, the *Alabama* had gained her fame by defeating 68 Union ships.

Who would not surrender?

Under the command of Captain James Iredell Waddell, the Confederate ship *Shenandoah* roamed the Atlantic Ocean sinking Union shipping. Waddell ignored messages saying the war was over and continued fighting. He did not surrender until seven months after the South's surrender.

What snake set out to strangle the South?

"Scott's Anaconda Plan" was the nickname given to the North's naval blockade of the South. It was designed to work like a great snake, strangling the South by cutting off its supplies, and was suggested by General Winfield Scott.

Was the Civil War fought only on land?

No, Union ships blockaded the South, preventing supplies getting in and the valuable export of cotton. Confederate raiders fought back by attacking the North's merchant shipping. The North's powerful navy grew to 670 ships; the South's to 130.

How did the Mississippi River help the North?

By controlling the Mississippi River, which divided the South into two, the Union was able to contain the fighting within a certain area. It was also able to supply its troops by running ships up and down the river.

What was the torpedo service?

Created by the South in October 1862, the torpedo service was responsible for laying mines—called "torpedoes"—in harbors and rivers. The mines sank 43 Union ships. The most common "Rains" torpedoes (named after their inventor) were made from beer kegs.

What was the first big battle?

The first major engagement of the war took place on July 21, 1861, at Bull Run. The glory of war that some troops had imagined became a nightmare. A Union officer said of his troops: "They seemed to be paralyzed, standing with their eyes and mouths wide open, and did not seem to hear me." The Union suffered a surprise defeat, and realized that a quick victory would not be theirs.

Who was Elmer E. Ellsworth?

The famous 24-year-old colonel was the first officer to die in the war. He led the first Union troops to march South. When he was shot by an innkeeper while taking down a Confederate flag in Alexandria, the North was outraged.

What happened at Fort Sumter?

Confederate artillery started bombarding the Union's Fort Sumter, near Charleston Harbor, on April 12, 1861. The following day, the fort commander surrendered. More importantly, the attack had signaled the start of the war.

Charleston Harbor after the bombing

What did it mean to "see the elephant"?

"Seeing the elephant" was the troops' phrase for fighting the enemy for the first time. It must have been a terrifying experience. The phrase was perhaps taken from farm boys, who expressed wonder at "seeing the elephant" after visiting the circus for the first time.

How did General Thomas J. Jackson become known as "Stonewall"?

General Jackson became Lee's right-hand man in the war. At Bull Run, a Confederate general rallied his troops by pointing at Jackson and crying: "There stands Jackson like a stone wall! Rally behind the Virginians!"

Who panicked at Bull Run?

Amazingly, the battle was watched by sightseers, including some congressmen, who had traveled down in buggies from Washington. Dressed in their fine clothes, they set up picnics near the battlefield so they could watch the 75,000 troops do battle. When the Union forces started their retreat, the spectators panicked, causing a rout that reached almost as far as Washington.

What did Confederate troops hope to capture at Honey Springs?

Slaves. The Confederates took slave shackles with them into battle at Honey Springs on July 17, 1863, because they were fighting against black Union troops whom they expected to capture. In fact, this battle in Indian Territory was won by the 1st Kansas Colored Volunteers.

"Stonewall" Jackson was seen as a brave leader of men.

Who killed "Stonewall" Jackson?

At the Battle of Chancellorsville, Jackson was mistakenly shot by his own troops. He had to have an arm amputated, and died—like many soldiers—from illness caused by his wounds.

What was the bloodiest day of the war?

The forces of General Lee and General McClellan met at Antietam Creek, near the town of Sharpsburg, on September 17, 1862. In the single bloodiest day of the war, 13,724 Confederate and 12,410 Union soldiers were killed or wounded.

What famous battles were fought in the first part of the war?

Important battles and campaigns included Bull Run (July 21, 1861), the Seven Days' Battles (June 25 to July 1, 1862), Antietam Creek (September 17, 1862), Fredericksburg (December 13, 1862), and Chancellorsville (May 1–5, 1862).

Generals and commanders often viewed the battles from a safe distance.

What was the Gettysburg Address?

So many men died at Gettysburg that a cemetery covering 17 acres was created there. When Lincoln dedicated it on November 19, 1863, he made one of the most famous speeches in American history—the Gettysburg Address.

The Gettysburg Address is still known as one of the greatest speeches of all time.

What was the Battle of Gettysburg?

Gettysburg was the most famous battle ever fought on American soil. An army of 75,000 Confederate soldiers attacked 87,000 entrenched Union troops at the market town of Gettysburg, Pennsylvania, from July 1 to 3, 1863. When the South's charge on the final day was cut down, any hope for a Confederate victory in the war was lost.

How many soldiers died at Gettysburg?

General Lee may have lost up to 25,000 men, while General Meade lost 23,000. Some regiments were virtually wiped out. The 26th North Carolina Infantry lost 708 dead and wounded out of a total of 800 men.

Three Confederate soldiers captured during the Battle of Gettysburg

Who were the commanding officers at Gettysburg?

The Union forces were commanded by General George Meade. During the battle he was said to be "quick, bold, cheerful, and hopeful." The Confederates were commanded by Robert E. Lee, who repeated sadly after Pickett's charge: "It's all my fault."

Who put his own bones in a museum?

Major General Daniel Sickles was a Union general who was struck by a cannonball at Gettysburg. His leg had to be amputated, and he instructed the bones to be sent to the Army Medical Museum, where he visited them for many years.

What famous battles were fought in the later part of the war?

Famous engagements and campaigns included the capture of Vicksburg (July 4, 1863), Chickamauga (September 19–20, 1863), the Battle of the Wilderness (May 5–6, 1864), and the Siege of Petersburg (June 1864–April 1865).

What was Pickett's charge?

Twelve thousand infantrymen slowly advanced in a straight line under General George Pickett right into the mouths of the Union artillery. As they advanced, the Union artillery cut them down in their thousands. It made a noise "strange and terrible, a sound that came from thousands of human throats ... like a vast mournful roar." When Pickett was asked to reorganize his division, he replied: "General Lee, I have no division now."

Who died without firing a shot?

Some of the soldiers at Gettysburg were completely untrained and had never even fired a rifle in action. After the battle, many single-shot rifles were found stuffed with up to ten charges. Their owners had kept reloading them without ever managing to fire them.

Why did the men of Pickett's charge stop advancing?

Even as the cannonballs flew among them, the soldiers stopped to make sure that their line was straight. One of the Union soldiers mumbled in horrified disbelief: "My God! They're dressing the line."

What happened after the Confederates surrendered?

After turning in their arms, Confederate soldiers were simply left to make their own way home. The roads were soon crowded with them. Ships and trains carried the Union troops to their home states, where they were paid and discharged.

What happened to captured soldiers?

Many captured soldiers on both sides were kept in terrible prison camps. Andersonville prison in Georgia was the worst of these. Nearly one in three of the Union soldiers held there— a total of more than 13,000 men—died from starvation and disease. Photographs taken of prisoners who somehow survived show the terrible effects of starvation. Former inmates of one prison weighed less than 100 lbs (45 kg).

How many soldiers died in prison?

About 194,000 Union soldiers were held prisoner, and 30,000 of them died. Some 214,000 Confederate soldiers were held in prison camps in the North, where 26,000 died.

Confederate soldiers returning home

What is Providence Spring?

At Andersonville prison, the drinking water was filthy. But in August 1864, after a rainstorm, a spring of pure, clean water bubbled up from the ground. The prisoners, believing it was a sign that God had not forgotten them, called it Providence Spring. It still flows today.

What horror happened on board *The Sultana*?

The Sultana was a paddle steamer designed to carry 370 passengers. On April 24, 1865, it left Vicksburg with 2,000 freed Union prisoners aboard. When its boiler exploded, 1,700 men who had survived the horrors of prisoner-of-war camps perished in the blazing inferno.

General William Tecumseh Sherman, the "Vandal Chief"

How many battles were there?

The war lasted for 1,489 days from the capture of Fort Sumter on April 12, 1861 until the last battle at Palmito Ranch on May 12, 1865 (about a month after General Lee's surrender). During this time there were over 10,000 engagements.

Which vandal led the "March to the Sea"?

At the end of 1864, the North's Major General William Tecumseh Sherman led his troops through Georgia from Atlanta to the coast. The "Vandal Chief" used a new form of warfare, burning or seizing property to break the will of the civilian population.

Where did General Lee finally surrender?

At 3:00 p.m. on Palm Sunday, April 9, 1865, Lee signed the surrender at the courthouse in Appomattox, Virginia. Under the terms agreed with General Grant, all Confederate soldiers could return home without facing trial for treason. Lee also made a special request that those cavalrymen with their own horses might be allowed to take them back to their homes.

Who was Henry Wirz?

Captain Henry Wirz was the Swiss commander of the prison at Andersonville. The press named him the "Andersonville Savage." After a show trial he was found guilty of war crimes and hanged in front of a huge crowd.

How many soldiers died in the Civil War?

During the Civil War, 620,000 men lost their lives—more than in all the United States' other wars combined. Of these, 60 percent died from disease. As a comparison, in World War II, 405,000 American troops lost their lives.

What operation was most often performed on the battlefield?

Three out of four operations performed in the field hospitals were amputations. The bullets fired by civil war rifles inflicted terrible damage. Surgeons regarded amputation as the only way to stop disease spreading in badly injured limbs. But their equipment was never sterilized, and it was quite rare for a surgeon to wash his hands or instruments between operations.

Amputations were common, but many died from infected wounds as a result of the operation.

Who was Clara Barton?

Clara was a New England woman who worked in a patent office. She placed an advertisement in a newspaper asking for medical supplies, which she then carried to the battlefield. There she provided a soup kitchen and offered bandages and medicines to the wounded. After the war, in 1881, she founded the American Red Cross. A senator said: "She has the talent of a statesman, the command of a general, and the heart and hand of a woman."

Clara Barton helped many wounded soldiers.

How were quinine and morphine smuggled to the troops?

Women and children sometimes smuggled precious medical supplies from the North to the South inside dolls with hollow heads and bodies.

Which side had the best medical services?

All the major pharmacies were located in the North. In 1863, two government laboratories were set up employing chemists and 350 workers to make medicines and pills.

What did Louisa May Alcott say about hospitals?

The famous author of *Little Women* worked as a Union nurse in the war. She wrote: "A more perfect pestilence box than this I never saw—cold, damp, dirty, full of vile odors from wounds, kitchens, and stables."

Why were casualties so high?

The soldiers in the Civil War were disadvantaged in the battles they fought. Advances in weapons meant that the ability to kill and wound had suddenly increased, but the surgeon's ability to mend and heal had not yet entered the modern age.

Were any drugs used successfully?

To treat malaria, doctors had quinine, which is still used today. Opium was an effective painkiller, but soldiers who took it became addicted. Chloroform was used as an anesthetic.

Hospitals were often makeshift and unhygienic.

What were hospital standards like in 1861?

Doctors had no antibiotics, no understanding of bacteria or sterilization, and no knowledge of the connection between filthy water and disease. If patients survived their wounds, they were likely to die from typhoid, dysentery, or pneumonia.

What happened to Robert E. Lee?

He became president of Washington College (now Washington and Lee University) in Lexington, Virginia. After his defeat, he said: "I believe it to be the duty of everyone to unite in the restoration of the country, and the establishment of peace and harmony."

What did John Wilkes Booth do at the theater?

On the evening of Good Friday, April 14, 1865, the actor rushed into Lincoln's box at Ford's Theater and fired a single pistol shot into the President's head. He then leapt from the box, breaking his leg but still managing to escape. Lincoln died the following morning. Booth was later killed. An outspoken advocate of slavery, Booth was part of the militia that hanged abolitionist John Brown before the war began.

Why did Lincoln not want to go to the theater?

Lincoln had had a dream in which he foresaw his own death. In this dream, which he recounted to his wife, he saw himself lying in his coffin.

Lincoln was shot in this box at Ford's Theater.

Lewis Payne, one of Booth's associates, was arrested for the murder of Lincoln.

What was Jefferson Davis wearing when he was captured?

When he was captured by Union cavalry on May 10, 1865, Davis was emerging from a tent wearing a shawl given to him by his wife. This led to stories in the North that he had been trying to escape dressed in skirts and a bonnet.

When did the Civil War end slavery?

Officially, according to the Emancipation Proclamation that Lincoln had made during the war, it ended on January 1, 1863.

What did Walt Whitman write about Lincoln's funeral?

He wrote the famous poem *When lilacs last in the dooryard bloom'd*, which includes the verse: "With the tolling, tolling bells' perpetual clang, Here, coffin that slowly passes, I give you my sprig of lilac."

What was the Ku Klux Klan?

After the war, a secret society was formed, whose members wore masked uniforms, named shrouds, and burned crosses. Among the new members was cavalry hero Nathan Bedford Forrest.

What were "carpetbaggers"?

This was the name given to Northerners who traveled to the South to try to influence how the defeated states should be run. The term suggested that they turned up in the South with only enough possessions to fill the cheap suitcase known as a carpetbag. Some carpetbaggers went South to make money, some for political office, and some to ensure the black population used the power to vote that they had been given.

How did the Civil War affect the game of baseball?

Union soldiers from New York City played the game wherever they went. The rules gradually spread around the battlegrounds, and after the war the sport began to gain great popularity.

Union soldiers playing baseball during the Civil War.

Presidents

Where does the president live?

The president's official home address is 1600 Pennsylvania Avenue, Washington, D.C., commonly known as the White House. As well as private rooms for the president and his family, the White House also has dozens of public function rooms and government offices. Since 1800, when the second president, John Adams, moved in with his wife, Abigail, and their family, all of the presidents have lived at the White House.

What is a presidential term?

A "term" is the time that a president stays in office. The term ends exactly four years later.

What does being president entail?

The president is in charge of the United States of America. His list of jobs includes being head of the government administration and foreign policy. He chooses people to head government departments (the Secretaries of State, the Treasury, Defense, and so on), and he is Commander-in-Chief of the U.S. Army and U.S. Navy.

Who can be president?

A candidate has to be at least 35 years old, a natural citizen of the U.S., and must have lived in the U.S. for at least 14 years. He or she has to be elected, too!

The White House was burnt down during the British invasion in 1814, and rebuilt in the 1820s.

The president's airplane has to be very secure, and requires the latest technology to keep the president in touch with his staff.

What is Air Force One?

The airplane that the president and the White House staff use when they travel on official business is called Air Force One. It is operated by the U.S. Air Force, and is currently a Boeing 747.

Who is the first lady?

The first lady is the president's wife. Traditionally, she organizes functions and acts as hostess at the White House. She also involves herself in social issues and charities.

Who chooses the president?

The people of the United States! In the November of the year before a presidential term ends, the people in each state vote for people called "electors." The electors then vote for the presidential candidates from each political party. The candidate who gains the majority of votes wins.

What does the vice-president do?

The vice-president is elected along with the president as his "running mate"—a sort of second-in-command. The vice-president acts as president of the Senate. In the event of the president dying in office, the vice-president takes over as president.

How long can a person be president?

The maximum time that a president can serve for is two full terms, or eight years. Then he or she must step down. This rule was introduced in 1951.

What goes on inside the Oval Office?

The Oval Office is the president's formal office in the West Wing of the White House, where he confers with heads of state and deals with the issues of the day.

Will there ever be a first man?

There is no reason why not, since there is nothing to prevent a woman from becoming president.

Who was the first president of America?

Georrge Washington was elected first president in 1789. Prior to that, he was elected commander-in-chief of the Continental army, which fought against, and beat, the British in the American Revolution. After the war was over, the United States was formed as an independent country. Washington was president for two terms in office. He died in 1799 from a throat infection.

Which president was never elected?

Gerald Ford. He became vice-president in 1973, when Vice-president Agnew resigned. He became President Ford in 1974, when President Nixon himself resigned.

Which president lost but won?

In the 1888 election, Benjamin Harrison, from Indiana, received 100,000 fewer popular votes than his opponent, Grover Cleveland, but carried the Electoral College 233 to 168, allowing him to become the 23rd president of the U.S.

How many presidents have there been?

Up to and including George W. Bush, there have been 43 presidents of the U.S. They are:

1	1789	George Washington (1732–1799)
2	1797	John Adams (1735–1826)
3	1801	Thomas Jefferson (1743–1826)
4	1809	James Madison (1751–1836)
5	1817	James Monroe (1758–1831)
6	1825	John Quincy Adams (1767–1848)
7	1829	Andrew Jackson (1767–1845)
8	1837	Martin Van Buren (1782–1862)
9	1841	William Henry Harrison (1773–1841)
10	1841	John Tyler (1790–1862)
11	1845	James Knox Polk (1795–1849)
12	1849	Zachary Taylor (1784–1850)
13	1850	Millard Fillmore (1800–1874)
14	1853	Franklin Pierce (1804–1869)
15	1857	James Buchanan (1791–1868)
16	1861	Abraham Lincoln (1809–1865)
17	1865	Andrew Johnson (1808–1875)
18	1869	Ulysses Simpson Grant (1822–1885)
19	1877	Rutherford Birchard Hayes (1822–1893)
20	1881	James Abram Garfield (1831–1881)
21	1881	Chester Alan Arthur (1830–1886)
22	1885	Grover Cleveland (1837–1908)
23	1889	Benjamin Harrison (1833–1901)
24	1893	Grover Cleveland (1837–1908)
25	1897	William McKinley (1843–1901)
26	1901	Theodore Roosevelt (1858–1919)
27	1909	William Howard Taft (1857–1930)
28	1913	Woodrow Wilson (1856–1924)
29	1921	Warren Gamaliel Harding (1865–1923)
30	1923	Calvin Coolidge (1872–1933)
31	1929	Herbert Clark Hoover (1874–1964)
32	1933	Franklin Delano Roosevelt (1882–1945)
33	1945	Harry S Truman (1884–1972)
34	1953	Dwight David Eisenhower (1890–1969)
35	1961	John Fitzgerald Kennedy (1917–1963)
36	1963	Lyndon Baines Johnson (1908–1973)
37	1969	Richard Milhous Nixon (1913–1994)
38	1974	Gerald Rudolph Ford (1913–)
39	1977	James Earl Carter (1924–)
40	1981	Ronald Wilson Reagan (1911–2004)
41	1989	George Herbert Walker Bush (1924–)
42	1993	William Jefferson Clinton (1946–)
43	2000	George Walker Bush (1946–)

George Washington declined a third term as president.

Under President Van Buren, the U.S. went to war with the Seminole Indians.

Who was the first all-American president?

Martin Van Buren was the first president to be born an American citizen. The presidents before him were born before the Declaration of Independence in 1776, and so were officially British citizens.

Which presidents were also vice-presidents?

Adams, Jefferson, Van Buren, Nixon, Ford, and Bush, who were later elected president; and Tyler, Fillmore, Andrew Johnson, Arthur, Theodore Roosevelt, Coolidge, Truman, and Lyndon Johnson, who took over on the deaths of their presidents.

Who was the youngest president?

Theodore Roosevelt, the 26th president. He was elected vice-president in the 1900 elections and became president in September 1901, after the assassination of President McKinley. He was just 42 years old at the time. He was easily reelected in 1904 for a second term that began in 1905.

Which presidents resigned from office?

Only President Richard Nixon, on August 9, 1974, halfway through his second term. He resigned because of the Watergate Affair.

Which state has produced the most presidents?

Virginia, where nine presidents were born, including four of the first five. Next comes Ohio, with seven. President Clinton was the first president from Arkansas.

Who was reelected the most times?

Franklin Delano Roosevelt was the only president to be elected three times (in 1932, 1936, and 1940). He was then elected again in 1944, making it a record four times.

Theodore Roosevelt won the Nobel Peace Prize in 1906 for trying to help resolve the Russo-Japanese war.

Who was the youngest elected president?

In 1961, John F. Kennedy, at age 43, was the youngest man ever to be elected president. (In 1901, Theodore Roosevelt, at age 42, was the youngest man ever to become president.)

Who was elected again after defeat?

President Grover Cleveland is the only president to have served two terms separated by another presidency (that of Benjamin Harrison, who served from 1889 to 1893).

Who was president most briefly?

The 9th president, William Henry Harrison. He was in office from March 4 to April 4, 1841. Harrison was 68 years old when he was inaugurated, but sadly he died from pneumonia exactly one month later.

Franklin D. Roosevelt lost the use of his legs as a result of an illness, polio, in 1921.

Who was president for the longest time?

Franklin Delano Roosevelt, who held office for more than 12 years. He became president in 1933, and again in 1937. In 1941 he became the only person to be president for a third term. In 1944 he was elected again, but died suddenly after he gained office in 1945.

Who was the oldest president?

Ronald Reagan, who was 69 years old when he was inaugurated in January 1981. Reagan was reelected in 1984, and was 77 years old when he left office in 1989.

Who invented the cabinet?

The cabinet is a committee made up of the heads of the government departments. It was George Washington's idea. Originally it had just four members—the Secretaries of State, the Treasury, War, and the Attorney General.

Who made the United States twice as big?

In 1803, President Jefferson bought an area of land known as the Louisiana Territory from France. It stretched from the Mississippi River to the Rocky Mountains, and cost just $15 million.

Which president helped abolish slavery?

Abraham Lincoln. Slavery was the main reason for the Civil War (1861–1865), between the Northern states (the Union), which wanted slavery abolished, and the Southern states (the Confederacy), which wanted to keep slavery. Lincoln was president of the victorious Union during the war.

Who was the Great Conservationist?

Theodore Roosevelt, the 26th president. He warned people about the dangers of using up the world's natural resources, and established the first wildlife refuge at Pelican Island, Florida.

Jefferson was a good scholar and was the main writer of the Declaration of Independence.

The CIA was linked with the Watergate scandal and was criticized by many people.

CENTRAL INTELLIGENCE AGENCY

UNITED STATES OF AMERICA

Who had a hotline to Russia?

In the early 1960s, President Kennedy called for an end to the Cold War between the West (led by the United States) and the East (led by the former Soviet Union, often called Russia). A special telephone line was connected between the White House in Washington and the Moscow Kremlin—the residence of the Soviet leader—so that the leaders could talk in times of crisis.

Who started the CIA?

The CIA (Central Intelligence Agency) was formed during the administration of President Harry S Truman in 1947. Its job is to collect and interpret information about other countries. In the past it has been accused of interfering in the internal affairs of countries, including the United States.

Who signed SALT for peace?

SALT is short for Strategic Arms Limitation Talks. These were negotiations between the United States and the former Soviet Union to stop production of nuclear missiles. SALT I (1972) was signed by President Nixon and Soviet leader Leonid Brezhnev. SALT II (1979) was signed by Leonid Brezhnev and President Carter.

Which president led a revolution?

Before becoming the first president of the United States, George Washington was an army officer. During the American Revolution against the British, General Washington led the Continental army, which he turned from a band of farmers into a fighting force. After five years of fighting, the turning point of the war came in 1781, when the main British force surrendered at Yorktown.

When were there two presidents?

During the Civil War (1861–1865), 11 southern states left the United States (the Union) to form the Union of Confederate States (the Confederacy). Abraham Lincoln was president of the Union, while Jefferson Davis was president of the Confederacy.

Washington was a distinguished soldier who coordinated his generals well against the British.

Who lost seven states?

James Buchanan, who was president before Abraham Lincoln. Near the end of his presidency, the states of Alabama, Florida, Georgia, Louisiana, Mississippi, South Carolina, and Texas left the Union before the start of the Civil War.

... and who got them back?

Abraham Lincoln, president of the victorious Union side during the Civil War. He was assassinated a few days after the war ended.

Who lost the White House in 1812?

The War of 1812 (which lasted from 1812 to 1815) was fought between the United States and Britain. In 1814, President James Madison fled from the White House before it was captured and burned out by the British.

Who won a war with Mexico?

James Knox Polk. He was president during the Mexican War (1846–1848), and fought over the position of the border between Mexico and the United States. The United States won half of Mexico.

Andrew Jackson became a hero after defeating the British at New Orleans.

Who reinforced the East Coast?

In 1823, President James Monroe announced that the United States would not put up with any more European interference in America. He supervised the construction of a chain of defenses on the East Coast of the United States to resist invasions.

Which hero was named Old Hickory?

Andrew "Old Hickory" Jackson. As Major General Jackson, he led a force of volunteers to victory against the Creek Indians in 1814. He also defeated the British in the Battle of New Orleans in 1815.

Who declared war on Spain?

The 25th president, William McKinley. He declared war on Spain in 1898, because the Spanish would not leave Cuba. The United States won the war after defeating Spain in both sea and land battles.

Who led the U.S. into World War II?

Which president declared war in 1917?

President Woodrow Wilson ordered U.S. ships to be armed against attacks by German submarines in March 1917. War was declared in April.

Japan attacked the U.S. naval base at Pearl Harbor, Hawaii, in 1941, and President Franklin D. Roosevelt immediately declared war in response. Roosevelt was president and commander-in-chief of the U.S. armed forces until he died shortly before the end of the war.

Who authorized that nuclear bombs should be dropped on Japan?

Harry S Truman took over as president in 1945, when World War II was still being fought. Truman authorized two nuclear bombs to be dropped on Japanese cities to force the Japanese to surrender quickly.

The Japanese Imperial Navy and a striking force of 353 aircraft attacked Pearl Harbor at 8:00 a.m. on Sunday, December 7, 1941. Approximately 100 ships of the U.S. Navy were present.

Who became president in an airplane?

Lyndon B. Johnson took over as president when President Kennedy was assassinated in Dallas in 1963. Johnson took the oath of office on board Air Force One in Dallas before returning to Washington, D. C.

Who shot down a U-2?

During the Cold War, a U-2 spy 'plane of the U.S. Air Force was shot down over the Soviet Union. The pilot of the U-2 was Francis Gary Powers. President Eisenhower defended the flight, saying that it was necessary for national security.

What was the Bay of Pigs?

In 1961, President Kennedy approved a plan for the CIA to help Cuban refugees invade Cuba and overthrow communist leader Fidel Castro. The invasion failed at the Bay of Pigs on Cuba's southern coast.

Images on television showed the people of the U.S. the true horror of what was happening in Vietnam, and the war became very unpopular.

Who sent troops to Vietnam?

In the mid-1960s, President Johnson sent nearly half a million troops to South Vietnam to fight against communist attacks from North Vietnam. The troops were withdrawn by President Nixon in the early 1970s, after fierce protests against the war.

Who ended the crisis in Cuba?

In 1962, there were rumors that the Soviet Union was putting nuclear missiles on Cuba. The Soviets withdrew when President Kennedy promised that the U.S. would not invade Cuba.

Who stayed away from the Olympics?

After the Soviet Union invaded Afghanistan in 1979, President Carter protested by ordering a boycott of the 1980 Moscow Olympics. Sixty-three other nations joined the boycott and refused to attend.

Who made war in the Gulf?

After Iraqi forces invaded Kuwait in 1990, President Bush announced the start of operation Desert Shield to protect neighboring countries in the Persian Gulf. In 1991, U.S. troops led operation Desert Storm to recapture Kuwait.

Who shot President John F. Kennedy?

What happens if a president dies in office?

The vice-president is immediately sworn in as president. The new president then selects a new vice-president.

Lee Harvey Oswald ... probably. President Kennedy was shot and killed while driving in a motorcade through Dallas on November 22, 1963. Lee Harvey Oswald, a former marine and a communist, denied firing the gun, but was shot himself before he could be tried. Many people believe that Oswald was not the killer, or at least that he did not act alone.

Nobody really knows who Jack Ruby was or why he killed Lee Harvey Oswald, but there are many theories.

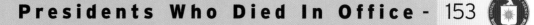

Has a president ever survived being shot?

Yes. Two in fact—Andrew Jackson and Ronald Reagan. In 1835, a man fired two guns at Jackson, but neither discharged. Jackson had a lucky escape, as both weapons were later found to be in working order. In 1981, John Hinckley shot Reagan in the chest. Reagan was lucky to survive.

Is there a new election after a president's death?

No. The vice-president is elected in partnership with the president, and voters know that he or she could become president. He or she serves for the remainder of the presidential term.

Which president survived a duel?

Andrew Jackson. In a duel in 1806 with Charles Dickinson, a local lawyer, Jackson was shot in the chest. The bullet was never removed. Dickinson died in the duel.

Who shot President Kennedy's killer?

Two days after President Kennedy was killed, Lee Harvey Oswald was shot at point-blank range by night-club owner Jack Ruby. Oswald was being moved to prison at the time he was shot.

Just five days after Lincoln's victory in the Civil War, he was murdered.

Which president was shot in a theater?

Abraham Lincoln, the 16th president, was shot on April 14, 1865, at Ford's Theater, Washington, D.C. He died the next day. His assassin, John Wilkes Booth, shot him from behind in his theater box. Booth then leapt onto the stage, shouting, "The South is avenged!" (He was referring to the Civil War, in which the South was defeated.) Booth was shot and killed while resisting arrest two days later.

Were any other presidents assassinated?

James Garfield and William McKinley were both assassinated. Garfield was shot on July 2, 1881, at Baltimore and Potomac station in Washington, D.C. He died two months later from blood poisoning caused by operations to remove the bullet. McKinley was shot on September 6, 1901, and died eight days later from gangrene.

Which other presidents died in office?

Four presidents died of natural causes while in office. They were William Henry Harrison, Zachary Taylor, Warren G. Harding, and Franklin D. Roosevelt.

What did Eisenhower plan in Europe?

Dwight D. Eisenhower joined the army during World War I and served until 1948. In 1943, during World War II, he became a general and was given the title of Supreme Allied Commander. He was ordered to plan Operation Overlord, the Allied invasion of Europe, which began with the D-day landings in France on June 6, 1944.

Who led the Union army in the Civil War?

Ulysses S. Grant. In 1862, he won the first major victory of the war against the Confederates and was promoted to major general. After more victories, he was made commander of all the Union armies in 1864.

Who beat the Shawnee Indians at Tippecanoe?

The Battle of Tippecanoe Creek took place in 1811. William Henry Harrison, then governor of Indiana, with a force of army regulars and militiamen fought off a surprise attack by an estimated 700 Shawnees.

Who won the Battle of New Orleans?

Andrew Jackson. During the War of 1812 (1812–1815), Jackson's troops defended the city of New Orleans from attack by highly trained British troops. There were 2,000 British casualties, including 291 killed, compared to just 21 Americans.

After military success in World War II, as president, Eisenhower used his skills to try to solve the Cold War situation.

General Taylor had little formal education, but was a well-respected soldier. He was awarded a Purple Heart medal due to being wounded by the enemy.

Who made his name fighting Mexicans?

Zachary Taylor, who fought in the Mexican–American War (1846–1848). In 1847, at Buena Vista, General Taylor's men fought and beat a much larger force of Mexicans. During the battle, two bullets went through Taylor's clothing. Taylor became a hero when news of the victory reached Washington. He later became the 12th president.

Who was the youngest pilot in the navy?

In 1943, George H. W. Bush earned his wings to become the youngest pilot in the navy. He flew 58 sorties in torpedo bombers against Japanese ships in the Pacific. He was shot down twice at sea, and won the Distinguished Flying Cross.

Who rode rough at Kettle Hill?

The Rough Riders were a cavalry regiment made up of volunteers. They were formed in 1898 to fight in the Spanish–American War (1898–1902). At Kettle Hill, Cuba, they made a brave charge, led by Colonel Theodore Roosevelt.

Why did Kennedy get a Purple Heart?

John F. Kennedy was commander of a patrol boat that was sliced in two by a Japanese destroyer in World War II. He saved his crew and swam to an island, towing an injured crewman with him. He was awarded a Purple Heart medal for bravery.

Who made a lucky escape from the French?

During the French and Indian War of 1753–1760, George Washington fought in the Virginia Militia. At Pittsburgh, four bullets went through his clothes and two horses were killed as he rode them.

What did 70 million people watch on TV?

The first televised election debate, which took place between John F. Kennedy and Richard Nixon—the opponents in the 1960 presidential election campaign. The two candidates appeared together on four live television debates.

The idea of two politicians debating on television caught the imagination of the U.S.

In which year was the Republican Party founded?

In 1854. Its first president was Abraham Lincoln. Between 1860 and 1928, all but two presidents were Republicans.

... and what about the Democratic Party?

The Democratic Party was formed in the 1790s. Confusingly, its members called themselves Democratic-Republicans at first.

Who had a tough job in Great Britain?

John Adams was appointed ambassador to Britain in 1785, just two years after America's independence from Britain was recognized. It was a tough job because he was the first ambassador, and there was still bad feeling between the countries. Adams returned to the United States in 1788, and was soon elected vice-president.

Who were the mugwumps?

Mugwumps were Republicans who deserted their own candidate, James Blaine, to help the campaign of Democrat Grover Cleveland, who was elected president in 1884.

James Polk may have been little known, but he was said to have brought about the Mexican War with his aggressive policies.

Who asked, "Who is James Polk?"

When the Democrats tried to choose their man for the 1844 presidential election, they found it impossible to decide between the candidates. Then James K. Polk entered the race and won. He was so little known that during the elections, members of the Whig party made fun of him, asking, "Who is James Polk?"

Who was the brains behind the Brains Trust?

The Brains Trust was a team of top advisors gathered together by Franklin D. Roosevelt. It helped him to win the 1932 election.

Which rich man pretended to live in a log cabin?

So that people would vote for him, William Henry Harrison's supporters portrayed him as a poor man, who lived in a small log cabin and drank cheap cider. In fact, he lived in luxury in a 22-room manor house.

Have all presidents been either Republicans or Democrats?

No. The Federalist party was supported by the first two presidents, George Washington and John Adams. In the mid-1800s, the Whigs had four presidents—William Henry Harrison, John Tyler, Zachary Taylor, and Millard Fillmore.

Which first lady is most famous?

Jackie Kennedy, later Onassis, was always in the media spotlight. She was a glamorous woman, much loved by the people of the U.S.

Probably Jacqueline Lee Bouvier (1929–1994), who became Mrs. Kennedy. She met John F. Kennedy in 1951, and they were married in 1953. After her husband's assassination, she married Greek shipping tycoon Aristotle Onassis in 1968.

Which presidents were related?

There have been four sets of related presidents. John Quincy Adams was one of four children of John Adams. Benjamin Harrison was one of thirteen children of John Scott Harrison, who was one of nine children of William Henry Harrison. Theodore Roosevelt was a fifth cousin of Franklin D. Roosevelt. George W. Bush is the oldest son of forty-first president George Bush Senior.

Which president married his cousin?

In 1905, Franklin D. Roosevelt married Eleanor Roosevelt, his fifth cousin once removed. She took an active part in politics, and after her husband's death she served as Chair of the United Nations Commission on Human Rights.

Who married a rich widow?

In 1759, George Washington married Martha Dandridge Custis, a widow with a large estate known as White House (not *the* White House). She was said to be the wealthiest widow in Virginia. In 1754 he inherited another fortune, his brother's large estate, called Mount Vernon.

Harry Truman came from a farming background. He became president in 1945, when Roosevelt died.

What did the S in Harry S Truman stand for?

Nothing! S was his middle name! Truman's parents could not decide between the names Shippe or Solomon, the names of his two grandfathers, so they chose to call him simply S instead.

Which presidential family of modern times is most famous?

It must be the Kennedys. John F. Kennedy's father, Joseph Patrick Kennedy, was a millionaire businessman by the age of 35. Two of his brothers entered politics. Robert F. Kennedy was attorney general and a senator. He was assassinated in 1968. Edward Kennedy is also a senator.

Who was born humbly at an inn?

Andrew Johnson was born in the winter of 1808 in a log cabin in the grounds of an inn, where his mother worked as a maid. He grew up in extreme poverty.

Who was the first poor president?

The first six presidents all came from well-off families. The father of the seventh, Andrew Jackson, was a poor farmer who had emigrated to the United States from Ireland, and died before Jackson was born.

When did a dog help a president?

While Richard Nixon was running for vice-president in 1952, he had to defend himself against a charge of accepting gifts of money while he was a senator. On television he gained public support by admitting to receiving just one gift—a dog named Checkers.

Who was married twice—to the same wife?

Andrew Jackson. In 1791 he married Rachel Donelson Robards, but the marriage was not legal because Rachel was not divorced from her first husband. They were remarried (properly this time) in 1794.

Who did better than his dad?

George W. Bush was elected for a second term as president of the United States in November 2004, defeating his Democrat challenger, John Kerry. His father, George Bush senior, lost to Bill Clinton when seeking a second term in office in 1992.

What was the Gettysburg Address?

The Gettysburg Address was a speech made by President Abraham Lincoln at the site of the Battle of Gettysburg, Pennsylvania, on November 19, 1863, just after the Civil War ended. It contained just 286 words, yet is one of the most famous speeches ever made. In it, Lincoln spoke of, "Government of the people, by the people, and for the people."

In 2004, George W. Bush won the popular vote for the presidency by a narrow margin, campaigning to continue the 'war on terror'.

Calvin Coolidge was known for his dry wit. As president, he earned a reputation for being honest, direct and hardworking.

Which president was really cool?

Calvin Coolidge. "Keep Cool with Coolidge" was the slogan used by the Republicans during the 1924 presidential election campaign.

How did George Washington keep the peace?

In his first speech to the American Congress, in 1790, President Washington said: "To be prepared for war is one of the most effectual means of preserving peace."

What was Kennedy's most famous saying?

In his inaugural address in 1961, John F. Kennedy said, "And so, my fellow Americans: Ask not what your country can do for you—ask what you can do for your country."

Who advised counting to 10?

Thomas Jefferson, the 3rd president of the United States. In his book entitled *A Decalogue of Canons for Observation in Practical Life,* he wrote: "When angry, count to 10 before you speak; if very angry, a hundred."

What did Wilson encourage fools to do?

Speak! In a speech in 1919, President Wilson said, "If a man is a fool, the best thing to do is to encourage him to advertise the fact by speaking."

What did Lincoln say about fooling people?

"You may fool all the people some of the time; you can even fool some of the people all the time; but you can't fool all of the people all the time."

Who advised carrying a big stick?

President Theodore Roosevelt's motto was: "Speak softly and carry a big stick; you will go far." He meant that you should use diplomacy, but be ready to use force if necessary.

Whose heads are carved into a mountain?

Four of the greatest American presidents are remembered at Mount Rushmore National Memorial in South Dakota. Huge heads of George Washington, Thomas Jefferson, Abraham Lincoln, and Theodore Roosevelt are carved into the granite of Mount Rushmore. The carving was started in 1927 and was eventually finished in 1941.

Who was known as General Mum?

William Henry Harrison. The name was given to him because he stayed mum (quiet) during the election campaign. He won because of the way his supporters criticized his opponent, Martin Van Buren.

Whose monument stands close to the White House?

The Washington Monument, dedicated to President George Washington. The obelisk stands 555 ft (170 m) high, and has a square base. It was built between 1848 and 1884. Visitors can take an elevator to the top.

Which president was sculpted in bronze?

Thomas Jefferson, the 3rd president and the man who drafted the Declaration of Independence. The Thomas Jefferson Memorial in Washington, D.C., is a classical monument with a bronze figure of Jefferson.

Most of the carving at Mount Rushmore was done by sculptor Gutzon Borglum. When he died in 1941, his son took over.

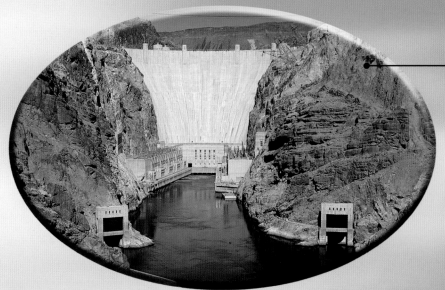

The Hoover Dam provides water for southern California, Arizona, and Mexico.

Who holds back water?

In 1947, the Boulder Dam on the Colorado River was renamed the Hoover Dam to honor President Herbert Hoover. At 726 ft (221 m), it is the highest concrete arch dam in the U.S.

Who was known as Old Man Eloquent?

John Quincy Adams. He earned the nickname after retiring as president and returning to Congress in the House of Representatives, where he served for 17 years.

Why are bears called "teddies"?

Theodore Roosevelt's nickname was Teddy. In 1902, while on a hunting trip in Mississippi, he refused to shoot a bear cub. This inspired a famous cartoon, which in turn inspired a toy called Teddy's bear.

Who was known as His Accidency?

John Tyler. He was vice-president to William Henry Harrison. When President Harrison died suddenly, Tyler took over. His opponents did not think he should be president, and called him His Accidency.

Which president is remembered at an airport?

John F. Kennedy International Airport, New York City, was named after President Kennedy.

Which president was never afraid?

President Lyndon B. Johnson said of Franklin D. Roosevelt, "He was the one person I ever knew, anywhere, who was never afraid."

Sporting Heroes

Who was the "father of football"?

Walter Camp, a player and coach at Yale. In the 1880s, he introduced many of the rules that are still used in the modern game. These included a system for scoring points, a team of 11 instead of 15 (as in rugby), the quarterback position, the line of scrimmage, and the idea that a team had to give up the ball if they did not advance by enough yards after a number of downs.

Walter Camp followed a strict regime of physical training and self denial, and was an outstanding all-round athlete.

Who invented lacrosse?

Lacrosse was invented in Canada by Native Americans, who called it "baggataway." Games played by the Iroquois tribe could last three days. There were up to 1,000 players on each team, and one of the aims was to disable as many of your opponents as possible. A modern version became the national sport of Canada and was introduced to the U.S. in 1868.

Who umpired and made the rules for the first real game of baseball?

A New York City surveyor named Alexander J. Cartwright developed 20 rules. In 1846, he umpired the first game using nine-player teams and a diamond with four bases. Fielders could run a batter out by tagging him, instead of by throwing the ball at him as in the British game of rounders.

What are "All-America" teams?

All-America teams are picked at the end of each season to indicate which college players have performed best in which position. The idea was pioneered by Walter Camp, who announced the first All-America football teams in 1889.

What did John Reid and six friends form in 1888?

They formed the United States' first golf club, St. Andrews, using a three-hole course in a New York cow pasture. The first member was Robert Lockhart, a linen merchant who had brought the clubs and balls back from Scotland.

When was the first great international boxing match?

It was fought with bare knuckles on April 17, 1860, between John C. Heenan of the U.S. and English champion Tom Sayers. The referee vanished when the crowd stormed the ring, and after 42 rounds it was called a draw.

What equipment was used to play the first game of basketball?

It was played using a soccer ball, with two peach baskets nailed to the walls of a YMCA gym. A ladder was used to retrieve the ball after a basket was scored. It was invented by Canadian James Naismith in 1891.

Who was Abner Doubleday?

According to legend, army cadet Doubleday invented baseball in the summer of 1839, in a cow field in Cooperstown, New York. The Baseball Hall of Fame was later built there to commemorate the event. In fact, the game played by Doubleday was more like the English game of rounders.

In 1839, Abner Doubleday is said to have devised the present-day playing positions of baseball.

What are the Queensberry Rules?

The Queensberry Rules are 12 rules of modern boxing, written in 1867 by John Graham Chambers and named for the Marquis of Queensberry. The rules introduced three-minute rounds, one-minute rests, the ten-second count, and gloves.

Who was baseball's first legend?

Adrian C. "Cap" Anson played first base from 1879.

Cap Anson, who made his debut in the new National League for the Chicago White Stockings (now White Sox) in 1876. Playing professional baseball for 27 years, he was the first player to make 3,000 hits. A candy bar and a cigarette were named after him, and a reporter wrote: "He stood at first base like a mighty oak ... the symbol of all that was strong and good in baseball."

When did baseball's Major Leagues begin?

Baseball's National League was founded in 1876. In 1900, the Western League was renamed the American League by its president, Ban Johnson. These two leagues became the Major Leagues.

Who was the first professional football player?

William "Pudge" Heffelfinger became the first professional football player when Allegheny Athletic Club paid him $500 to join them in 1892. Playing as a guard for Yale, he had been picked for the All-America teams for the previous three years.

Who was the "Boston Strong Boy"?

The great John L. Sullivan, who became the last World Heavyweight Boxing Champion of the bare-knuckle era by knocking out Paddy Ryan in nine rounds in 1882. He once won a 75-round fight in temperatures of up to 104°F (40°C). He was the first sporting hero to be paid to advertise products, and earned over $1 million during his career. Sport magazine called him: "A hero among heroes."

John L. Sullivan knocked out Paddy Ryan in the 9th round of the World Heavyweight Championship of 1882 in less than 11 minutes.

When was the first U.S. Open Golf Championship?

The first U.S. Open was played in 1895. When Fred Herd won the trophy in 1898, the United States Golf Association made him put down a deposit for the trophy. Golfers had such a bad reputation at that time that they thought he might pawn it!

How did Walker Breeze Smith win one of the United States' first golf matches?

He told his opponent, John C. Ten Eyck, that the secret was to keep your eye on the ball. He promptly removed his glass eye, balanced it on the ball, and teed off.

What did Harry Decker invent?

Decker was the inventor of the padded catcher's glove used in baseball. These gloves were known as "deckers" for many years.

Did Heffelfinger enjoy football?

It would appear so. William Heffelfinger was the first blocker to protect the ballcarrier by providing "interference." He spoke of "the fierce elation that comes from throwing your body across an opponent's knees and feeling him hit the turf with a solid crack."

How did the Civil War affect baseball?

During the Civil War, Union soldiers from New York City played the game wherever the fighting took them. As they traveled, they spread the rules used by the first real team, Alexander Cartwright's New York Knickerbocker Baseball Club.

Which hero of baseball made his debut in 1890?

Cy Young, who many consider to be the greatest pitcher ever, made his debut for Cleveland. Born Denton True Young, in Ohio, he went on to win an all-time record 511 Major League games during his career.

How did professional basketball develop?

The National Basketball League (NBL) was formed in 1898. It started as an attempt to find opponents who could take on the brilliant Trenton team of the YMCA League.

Cy Young claimed never to have been sick until he caught the flu at the age of 79.

What did Dr. Coburn Haskell invent in 1898?

Haskell, a dentist from Cleveland, was playing with a bundle of rubber bands when his idea struck him. He invented a golf ball, filled with twisted rubber bands, so it flew much farther than previous balls.

Gentleman Jim beat John L. Sullivan in 1892 for a purse of $25,000.

What did "Gentleman Jim" win in 1892?

"Gentleman Jim" Corbett knocked out John L. Sullivan in New Orleans to win the first World Heavyweight Championship fought with gloves under Queensberry rules. Sullivan, although unfit, made it to the 21st round before being knocked out.

How did Jim Corbett change boxing?

Corbett was known as the "father of scientific boxing" for his skill inside the ring. He was also nicknamed the "California Dandy" for his elegant appearance outside the ring. Both of these qualities helped to make boxing popular with the public.

Which great jockey invented the crouching position for riding?

Tod Sloan, from Indiana, invented the "monkey crouch." Having incredibly short legs, he found it more comfortable to ride with short stirrups and his body bent forward with his head almost on the horse's neck.

What prestigious medal did James B. Connolly receive in 1896?

Connolly received the first Olympic winner's medal awarded since Barasdates of Greece won the boxing in CE 393. The Olympics were revived at Athens in 1896 by Frenchman Baron Pierre de Coubertin, after a gap of 1,503 years. A triple jumper from Harvard, Connolly received a silver medal for winning. Gold was considered vulgar, and was not used for winners' medals until 1904.

Why did James B. Connolly almost not win his Olympic medal?

Connolly misunderstood the Greek calendar during the 1896 Olympics in Athens, Greece, and stayed up celebrating for the whole night before his historic track and field event.

Why was baseball's pitching mound moved from 50 ft (15 m) to 60 ft, 6 in (18.5 m) from the batter?

Amos Rusie, known as the "Hoosier Thunderbolt," was baseball's hardest-throwing pitcher of the 1890s. He pitched so fast that it was unfair on the batters, so the pitching mound was moved back. His catcher had to wear a sheet of lead in his glove to protect his hand.

Who appears on the most valuable baseball card?

Honus Wagner once said, "There isn't much to being a ballplayer, if you're a ballplayer."

Honus Wagner, the great Pittsburgh shortstop, who led the league in batting for eight seasons from 1900 to 1911. The 1909 card bearing his image was withdrawn because Wagner, who was against smoking, thought it set a bad example for children to see the cards in packs of cigarettes.

What did May Sutton wear to cause trouble at Wimbledon?

In 1905, because she was only 18 years old, May Sutton was allowed to wear a dress that did not cover her ankles. This glimpse of the Californian youngster's legs caused a lot of trouble at the All-England Club. Her tennis also upset the British, as she went on to become the first non-English player to win Wimbledon.

Who won a famous marathon by coming second?

Johnny Hayes, a sales clerk at Bloomingdales, finished 0.75 seconds behind Italian Dorando Pietri in the marathon at the London Olympics of 1908 in England. Pietri was disqualified, however, because British officials had helped him over the line after he collapsed!

In baseball, who won the first World Series?

The first World Series was played in 1903 between the winners of the National League and the new American League. Cy Young pitched the Boston Red Sox to a 5–3 victory over Pittsburgh.

Why was Cy Young perfect in 1904?

He pitched the first ever perfect game in baseball history, playing for the Boston Red Sox against the Philadelphia Athletics. Not a single Philadelphia batter reached first base on either a hit or a walk.

Why was a "Great White Hope" searched for?

The "Galveston Giant," Jack Johnson, became the first black World Heavyweight Champion by knocking out Tommy Burns in Sydney, Australia, in 1908. Johnson upset white society by hiring servants, buying a fleet of luxury cars, and twice marrying white women. So a desperate search began for a white boxer—a "Great White Hope"—who might beat him. Nobody succeeded until 1915.

Which Olympic champion lost out for refusing to jump on a Sunday?

Alvin Kraenzlein won his fourth winner's medal with a record-breaking long jump at the 1900 Paris Olympics in France. Previous record-holder Meyer Prinstein refused to compete because the event was held on a Sunday.

Why did Jack Johnson flee from the U.S. in 1912?

Johnson had been convicted of breaking a law by crossing state lines with his wife before they were married. Johnson fled, disguised as a member of a black baseball team, and defended his title abroad.

How did President Roosevelt change the game of football?

In 1905, President Roosevelt insisted that a bone-breaking, battering-ram formation called the "flying wedge" should once again be banned from the game (it was first banned in 1894). He did it after 18 players were killed in the previous season!

How did Charles Follis become the first black professional football player?

Follis agreed to join the Shelby team in exchange for being given a job in a hardware store in 1904. He became known as the "Black Cyclone," and was a major star of the Ohio League.

President Theodore Roosevelt was a great fan of football.

Who was Babe Ruth?

George Herman Ruth, from Baltimore, known as "Babe" and the "Sultan of Swat," was baseball's biggest-ever hero. A huge slugger, he shattered every batting record. His lifetime achievement of 714 home runs was not beaten until 1974, and his 60 homers in one season (1927) set one of sport's most famous records. Amazingly, he began his career as a pitcher. Even then, he set a World Series record of 29 consecutive scoreless innings for the Boston Red Sox.

Babe Ruth hit over 50 home runs in a season— four times!

Who became a football legend in only four years?

George Gipp, fullback for the famous Notre Dame college team. He became a national celebrity in a four-year career (1917–1920). Gipp died aged 25, after playing a game while sick with a temperature of 102°F (39°C).

What was the famous "Battle of the Camera Shot"?

The fight in which Jack Johnson was defeated by Jess Willard in 1915. Johnson claimed that a camera shot of him shading his eyes from the sun after his knockout proved that he had lost the fight deliberately and had not really been knocked out.

Who was the first woman to swim the English Channel?

Gertrude Ederle, daughter of a New York butcher. She won three swimming medals at the 1924 Olympics, and set nine world records. A violent storm blew up during her crossing on August 6, 1926. When her father asked from a boat if she wanted to quit, she said, "What for?" Her achievement was declared, "The greatest recorded athletic feat by a woman in the history of the world."

What did Frenchman Marshall Foch say about football?

Marshall Foch, the Frenchman who commanded the Allied Forces during World War I, said of a football game between the army and navy: "Mon Dieu, this game is war! It has everything."

What scandal shocked baseball fans in 1919?

The "Black Sox" scandal. After the Chicago White Sox lost the 1919 World Series to the Cincinnati Reds, eight players were accused of throwing the game for gamblers' money. They were acquitted, but were banned for life anyway.

Why was football running back Red Grange nicknamed the "Galloping Ghost"?

He seemed untouchable when carrying the ball. He once scored four touchdowns with his first four touches for Illinois University. Grantland Rice called him: "A gray ghost thrown into the game, that rival hands may rarely touch."

Who was "Shoeless" Joe Jackson?

A great baseball hitter, who once played in socks because his new shoes gave him blisters. He was the most popular player banned in the Black Sox scandal of 1919, causing the public to cry: "Say it ain't so, Joe!"

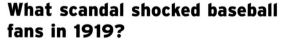

"Shoeless" Joe Jackson was one of the best hitters ever in baseball.

What did Mildred "Babe" Didrikson excel at?

This amazing Texan won the gold and set world records in the javelin and 80 meters hurdles at the 1932 Los Angeles Olympics. She received the silver in the high jump because her "western roll" style was judged illegal! She played on three championship basketball teams, toured playing billiards, and once pitched out Joe DiMaggio. Didrikson later helped establish the women's golf tour, winning the U.S. Women's Open three times.

How long did it take Jesse Owens to set three world records?

About 45 minutes. Between 3:15 and 4:00 p.m. on May 25, 1935, representing Ohio State University, Jesse Owens set world records in the 220 yards, the 220 yard hurdles, and the long jump.

Owens' long jump record was unbroken for 25 years, 79 days.

How was Hitler taught a lesson at the 1936 Berlin Olympics?

Hitler had hoped white athletes would demonstrate their racial supremacy. Black American athlete Jesse Owens, the 22-year-old son of a cotton picker, had other ideas. He broke three Olympic records and equaled another in winning gold in the 100 meters, 200 meters, long jump, and 4 x 100 meters relay. Hitler refused to present the medals. Owens remarked: "We lost no sleep over not being greeted by Adolf Hitler."

What was the first object to be placed in baseball's Hall of Fame?

When the Hall of Fame opened in 1936, the spikes of Ty Cobb, the first elected member, were put on display. Cobb was known for sharpening his spikes so that he could leave fielders a reminder of his presence.

Which golfer won the "Impossible Quadrilateral"?

In 1930, Bobby Jones became the only golfer ever to win the old Grand Slam—or "Impossible Quadrilateral," as it was called—of U.S. Amateur, U.S. Open, British Amateur, and British Open titles in one year.

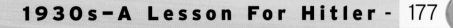

What baseball record did Lou Gehrig set?

Between June 1, 1925 and May 2, 1939, the "Iron Horse" of baseball played 2,130 consecutive games for the New York Yankees. He ignored broken fingers and pulled muscles to set a record that lasted until 1995.

Was Bronco Nagurski the toughest football player ever?

Possibly! The Chicago Bears fullback (1930–1937) once bulldozed through opponents for a 45-yard touchdown, collided with the goalposts, and ran on into a brick wall. Regaining consciousness, he said, "That last guy hit me awfully hard."

Why did President Roosevelt squeeze Joe Louis' biceps?

In 1938, Louis was fighting German champion Max Schmeling. With war looming, Roosevelt told him, "We need muscles like yours to beat Germany." Louis won in one round.

Who was the first sportsman to have a bigger salary than the President?

Baseball's Babe Ruth, who received $80,000 for the 1930 season. When asked why he deserved to earn more money than the President, Ruth said, "I had a better year!"

Who held the World Heavyweight boxing title for the longest time?

The brilliant "Brown Bomber" Joe Louis. He won the title from James Braddock in 1937, and held it for 11 years, 8 months. He defended the title 25 times, against a series of "Bum of the Month" challengers.

> Mildred Didrikson was nicknamed "Babe" after Babe Ruth, for hitting 13 home runs against a boys' team.

How did Sugar Ray Robinson get his name?

Walker Smith Jr. borrowed an identity card from his friend, Ray Robinson, so he could fight while under-age. He was called "sweet as sugar." As "Sugar Ray Robinson," he was possibly the greatest boxer of all time.

What was the "lace panties" scandal?

In 1949, "Gorgeous Gussy" Moran from California shocked Wimbledon by wearing a lace trim beneath a shorter-than-usual skirt. Designer Ted Tinling had to resign from his post as a Wimbledon official, but became famous as a dress designer.

Who was football's "Papa Bear"?

George Halas, who coached the Chicago Bears to a record 324 wins. In 1940, they scored a record NFL Championship victory of 73–0 against the Washington Redskins. At 66–0 they were asked not to convert a touchdown, because they had run out of balls!

Which golfing legend failed to win the U.S. Open?

Sam Snead won the 1946 British Open, three PGAs, and three Masters, but could never win the U.S. Open. He was runner-up four times—in 1947 missing a 30-inch putt on the last hole.

How did World War II affect sporting heroes?

Baseball stars enlisted, and the All-Star game was canceled in 1945. Some football teams stopped playing. The Pittsburgh Steelers and Philadelphia Eagles merged as the "Steagles" for one season. Hockey overtime was banned. More women and black players became stars.

From 1943 to 1951, Sugar Ray Robinson (right) won 91 consecutive fights.

Who was baseball's oldest-ever Major League rookie?

Satchel Paige, who was signed from the Negro Leagues by the Cleveland Indians in 1948, aged 42. A crowd of 72,000 watched his debut, and he went on to pitch in the Major League at the age of 59.

What did Simon and Garfunkel famously sing about Joe DiMaggio?

In the 1968 song *Mrs. Robinson*, they sang: "Where have you gone, Joe DiMaggio? / A nation turns its lonely eyes to you / What's that you say, Mrs. Robinson? / "Joltin" Joe has left and gone away."

Joe DiMaggio (shown left of Mickey Mantle) was known for his graceful style.

Which baseball legend married Marilyn Monroe?

"Joltin" Joe DiMaggio, the "Yankee Clipper," a legendary slugger and fielder. In 1941, he hit safely in a record 56 straight games—a run that almost ended when his brother nearly caught him! This winning streak led to one of the nine World Series DiMaggio won with the New York Yankees. He married fellow legend Marilyn Monroe in 1954, but they divorced a short time later.

What was the color barrier in baseball?

Black players were only allowed to play in the Negro Leagues, never in the Major Leagues. The unfairness of this situation became even clearer when black soldiers fought for the United States in World War II. The sporting hero who broke this barrier was Jackie Robinson, who signed for the Brooklyn Dodgers in 1947. He won the first Rookie of the Year award, despite some white players refusing to play against him.

Who was the first black woman to win Wimbledon?

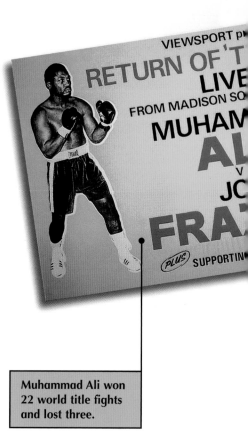

VIEWSPORT p

RETURN OF 'T
LIVE
FROM MADISON SO
MUHAM
A
v
JC
FRA
PLUS SUPPORTIN

Althea Gibson, who won the title in 1957. Gibson's talent had been spotted when she was a 13-year-old by a Police Athletic Supervisor, who bought her two secondhand rackets. She impressed in U.S. tournaments, where campaigns had to be staged to allow black players to compete. In her career, Gibson won two Wimbledons, two U.S. Championships, and one French title.

Muhammad Ali won 22 world title fights and lost three.

Why did Ben Hogan offer to have his lawnmower sent over to Britain?

Golf's "Ice Man" won one British Open, four U.S. Opens, two PGAs, and two Masters. When he won the British Open at Carnoustie, Scotland, he said of the long grass on the greens, "I've got a lawnmower back in Texas. I'll send it over."

Who was the only unbeaten heavyweight champion?

The "Brockton Blockbuster" Rocky Marciano. He won the title from Jersey Joe Walcott in 1952, and ended his career with 49 wins, 43 knockouts, and 0 losses—despite a short reach that meant he sometimes had to jump to land punches.

How did "Little Mo" get her name?

Big-hitting Maureen Connolly, who won tennis's Grand Slam in 1953, was named for "Big Mo"—the U.S. battleship *Missouri*. She won three U.S. Open titles and three Wimbledons before injury forced her into retirement at the young age of only 19.

Who was "The Greatest"?

Muhammad Ali claimed to be "The Greatest," and went on to become the most famous sportsman on the planet. In 1964, when he was still known as Cassius Clay, he defeated heavyweight champion Sonny Liston, who was believed to be unbeatable. Clay converted to Islam, and adopted his new name. As Muhammad Ali, he lit up sport with his boxing skills, predictions of victory, playful boasting, and famous poems such as his claim that he could, "Float like a butterfly, sting like a bee."

How did Muhammad Ali lose his world heavyweight title?

In 1967, he was stripped of his title for refusing to join U.S. conscription to fight in Vietnam. He said: "I don't have no quarrel with them Vietcongs."

Althea Gibson was 29 when she won her first Wimbledon title.

Did Roger Maris break Babe Ruth's record or not?

In 1961, Maris broke Ruth's hallowed record of 60 home runs in a season. However, he hit his 61st homer in the 162nd game, while Ruth's season lasted only 154 games. So, many people felt the Babe's record still stood.

Who collapsed in the 10th round of a 1952 Sugar Ray Robinson fight?

The referee! This fight against Joey Maxim at Yankee Stadium for the light-heavyweight championship was the only one in which Robinson was ever stopped. He retired with heat exhaustion in the 13th round.

Who lived in a penthouse with llama-fur carpets?

The flamboyant "Broadway" Joe Namath, the first quarterback to pass for 4,000 yards. In 1969, Namath promised that his New York Jets would beat hot favorites the Baltimore Colts in the Super Bowl. They did, 16–7.

What did Bobby Jones say about Jack Nicklaus?

Jones famously said of "Golden Bear" Nicklaus: "He plays a game with which I am not familiar." Nicklaus, possibly the greatest golfer ever, won three British Open, four U.S. Open, six Masters, and five PGA titles.

What did Mark Spitz achieve in 1972?

A t the Munich Olympics, the Californian swimmer won seven gold medals and set seven world records—two in freestyle, two in butterfly, and three in relays. As sport grew more commercial, Spitz retired and made money by advertising clothes, milk, hairdryers, and electric razors. He said of his seven golds, "The medals weighed a lot. They have heavy, crazy chains. Really, it was hard to stand up straight wearing them all."

Who gave her opponent a live pig?

Billie Jean King gave a pig to self-proclaimed male-chauvinist pig Bobby Riggs before their famous 1973 "Battle of the Sexes" tennis match. An audience of 50 million television viewers watched King defeat ex-pro Riggs. Billie Jean King had helped women's tennis to gain proper recognition by winning an amazing 20 Wimbledon titles during her career: six singles, 10 doubles, four mixed doubles.

Which athlete remained unbeaten for an amazing 10 years?

After victory in the World Cup 400 meters hurdles in 1977, Ed Moses won his next 122 races. During this time, he collected Olympic gold at Los Angeles in 1984 and broke the world record four times.

What were the "Rumble in the Jungle" and the "Thrilla in Manila"?

Two of Muhammad Ali's most famous fights. In the Rumble, in Zaire in 1974, Ali outwitted the enormous George Foreman to regain his title in eight rounds. In the Thrilla, in 1975, he defeated Joe Frazier.

Mark Spitz
swimming butterfly.

Connors was known for his powerful return of serve; Evert for her steady baseline play.

Which engaged couple won five Grand-Slam tennis events?

In 1974, 19-year-old Chris Evert won the French and Wimbledon titles. Her fiancé, 20-year-old Jimmy Connors, won the Wimbledon, U.S., and Australian titles. The couple split up at the end of the year.

Why was dunking banned from college basketball in 1968?

To try to reduce the dominance of player Lew Alcindor, who led UCLA to three college championships. After changing his name to Kareem Abdul-Jabbar, he broke all scoring records in helping the LA Lakers to five NBA championships.

How did Arthur Ashe prepare for his Wimbledon final?

By playing blackjack into the early hours. As a child, Arthur Ashe had been banned from tournaments in Virginia because of his color. In 1975, he beat Jimmy Connors to become the first black player to win the men's singles at Wimbledon.

Who was known as "The Juice"?

O. J. Simpson, one of the most graceful running backs ever. Playing for the Buffalo Bills in 1973, he shattered Jim Brown's rushing record, and became the first player to rush for 2,000 yards in a season.

Who is "Mr Hockey"?

Canadian Gordie Howe, who played 33 seasons of ice hockey, mainly for the Detroit Red Wings. He set the NHL record for points (1,850), won a WHA title playing alongside his two sons, and appeared in his 23rd All-Star game at the age of 51.

How did Carl Lewis win Olympic gold by coming second?

Carl Lewis stayed at the peak of condition for over 10 years.

In the 1988 Seoul Olympics in South Korea, Lewis was beaten in the 100 meters by Canadian Ben Johnson, who ran an astonishing 9.79 seconds. It was proved to be too astonishing—Johnson failed a drugs test and the gold went to Lewis.

Why did Carl Lewis wear red stilettos?

For a tyre advertisement! Lewis was possibly the athlete of the 20th century, with nine Olympic golds. He won four golds, broke the 100 meters Olympic record at the 1984 Games, and won the long jump in four consecutive Olympics.

Who is the highest-rated quarterback ever?

Joe Montana, who was named MVP in the NFL twice. He made the San Francisco 49ers the team of the '80s, winning four Super Bowls between 1982 and 1990. In the Championship game of 1982, he threw a famous play known as "The Catch." With a minute to play, losing 21–17, he threw a high pass to Dwight Clark for a touchdown. Montana said: "I don't know how he got it. He can't jump that high!"

Which ice hockey records does Wayne Gretzky hold?

Known simply as "The Great One," Gretzky dominated his sport more than any other team player in history. Playing for the Edmonton Oilers, and later the Los Angeles Kings, he was NHL scoring champion ten times and MVP nine times. In 1980, aged 19, he became the youngest player to be the season's top scorer. When he retired in 1999, he held records for career goals, points, and assists.

One of the best-ever quarterbacks was the great Joe Montana.

What did Reggie Jackson say about the World Series?

"The only reason I don't like playing in the World Series is I can't watch myself play." Jackson was called "Mr October" because of his outstanding record in World Series games—which are played in that month.

Which sisters-in-law won five golds at the 1988 Olympics?

Florence "Flo-Jo" Griffith-Joyner, famous for her multi-colored fingernails, won the gold in the 100 meters, 200 meters, and relay sprints. Her sister-in-law Jackie Joyner-Kersee won the gold in the heptathlon, with a world-record 7,291 points, and the long jump.

Why did '80s basketball star "Magic" Johnson retire in 1991?

He had been infected with the HIV virus. Combining height, speed, and skill, Johnson had transformed the position of guard, winning five championships with the LA Lakers, and setting a record for assists.

Who famously said: "You are the pits of the world!"?

Hot-tempered tennis genius John McEnroe, who won three Wimbledons and four U.S. Opens. In 1990, he became the first player to be disqualified from a Grand Slam tournament for verbally abusing an umpire.

Who lost only one tennis match in 1983?

Martina Navratilova, the Czech player who became a U.S. citizen in 1981. Navratilova set new standards for women's tennis, winning 18 major singles titles and a world-record 167 singles tournaments.

Nancy Kerrigan eventually won silver in figure skating at the 1994 Winter Olympics.

What happened before the 1994 Winter Olympics?

The ice skater was attacked and struck on the knee in an attempt to stop her competing. Her arch-rival Tonya Harding was accused of being involved and was later sentenced to three years' probation.

Which tennis star suddenly threw up on court?

"Pistol" Pete Sampras threw up on court during a fifth-set tiebreak against Alex Corretja, on his way to winning the U.S. Open in 1996. Sampras won Wimbledon six times in seven years, and has earned more than $32 million in prize-money.

What was the amazing "dream team"?

Because of changes in the rules, professionals could compete in the 1992 Barcelona Olympics. The U.S. won the basketball gold by forming a "dream team" of sporting heroes including Michael Jordan and "Magic" Johnson.

What did Greg Maddux and Pedro Martinez sign in 1997?

Maddux of the Atlanta Braves and Martinez of the Boston Red Sox each signed record contracts for $11.5 million a year. Maddux was the first player to win the Cy Young trophy for four consecutive years.

What happened in the 1997 Masters?

Tiger Woods became the youngest golfer to win the Masters, and the first black player to win a major tournament. Woods had already won $1 million in only nine tournaments. He not only won the Masters, but hit a record 18 under par, and won by an astonishing 12 shots. The tournament, which is held in Augusta, was founded by Clifford Roberts, who said, "As long as I'm alive, golfers will be white and caddies will be black."

Tiger Woods takes a shot.

Who is Mia Hamm?

Probably the best female soccer player ever. She scored 103 goals between 1989 and 1994—her university won four college championships and lost only one match. She played for the national team at the age of 15 and won a Women's World Cup winner's medal at 19.

Why was Mike Tyson disgraced and fined a record $2,980,000?

He bit off part of Evander Holyfield's ear during their bout in 1997. Holyfield will be remembered as a dignified champion. Tyson, who in 1986 became the youngest-ever heavyweight champ, aged 20, will unfortunately be remembered for this incident and a six-year prison sentence for rape.

Which sporting hero defied gravity?

Basketball's greatest player, Michael Jordan, who became known as "His Airness," because of his astonishing ability to change direction in mid-air. He won six NBA Championships with the Chicago Bulls, and was MVP in every final. Jordan had the highest-ever scoring average, won two Olympic golds, earned the most money in sporting history ($300 million), and appeared on *Sports Illustrated*'s cover a record 42 times (beating Muhammad Ali's total of 34).

What did George Foreman win in 1994?

At the age of 45, he became the oldest boxer to win a version of the world heavyweight title by defeating Michael Moorer. He said, "I proved that 40 is no death sentence."

What record did Mark McGwire shatter?

In 1998, he broke the record for home runs in a season. He hit 70 homers for the St. Louis Cardinals to overtake both Babe Ruth and Roger Maris.

What is the "House That Ruth Built"?

Yankee Stadium, built in 1923 with money from the audiences that Babe Ruth attracted. The Red Sox sold him to the New York Yankees for $125,000 in 1920. He led the Yankees to four World Series, and christened the new stadium with a home run.

Which sporting heroes went into show business?

Many of them! Jack Johnson ended his days performing with a flea circus; Jesse Owens raced against horses to make a living; and Jim Brown starred in the 1967 movie *The Dirty Dozen*.

Which sporting heroes have trophies named after them?

You know that you have become a sporting legend when a trophy is named after you. The Cy Young Award is given to each season's best pitcher. An award for best college football player is named after Walter Payton.

Who lit the torch for the 1996 Atlanta Olympics?

Muhammad Ali, in a ceremony made all the more moving because he was suffering from Parkinson's disease. Ali became the first man to twice regain the heavyweight title when he defeated Leon Spinks in 1978. A later comeback against Larry Holmes in 1980, in which Ali retired after 10 rounds of punishment, contributed to his illness. In Atlanta, he moved slowly and his hands shook, but he retained extraordinary dignity.

Why was Mildred Didrikson's last U.S. Open golf title so incredible?

She won by 12 strokes in 1954, only a year after having surgery for cancer. This remarkable sporting hero finally succumbed to the disease in 1956.

Which sporting hero faced a murder trial?

In 1994, O. J. Simpson was arrested, after a televised police chase, and charged with the brutal murder of his ex-wife Nicole Brown and her friend Ronald Goldman. Simpson had retired as a football player in 1979 and become a famous commentator and comic actor. His trial in 1995 was also televised, and attracted huge publicity. Simpson was controversially found not guilty.

O. J. Simpson was one of the sporting heroes of the 1970s.

Were Jim Thorpe's Olympic medals returned to his family?

At the 1912 Stockholm Olympics, Jim Thorpe won medals in the decathlon and pentathlon, but because he had been paid $2 a game to play baseball, he was not an amateur, and so the medals were taken back. In 1982, the International Olympic Committee (IOC) finally admitted that it had been wrong, and returned Thorpe's gold medals to his family. Thorpe had died penniless in 1953.

Why is the number 42 no longer worn by baseball players?

In 1997, Jackie Robinson's number—the number 42—was retired to celebrate the 50th anniversary of his breaking baseball's color barrier.

The Yankee Stadium is the home of baseball.

Great Americans

Who is one of the world's most famous preachers?

Baptist minister Billy Graham (born 1918) is probably the world's most famous evangelist. He has led preaching tours since 1944. On a tour in 1949, he preached to 350,000 people in Los Angeles and two million people in Madison Square Gardens, New York City.

Who were the suffragettes?

Suffragettes were people who campaigned for women to have the same rights as men. One of the most famous suffragettes in the U.S. was Elizabeth Cady Stanton (1815–1902), head of the National Woman's Suffrage Association. Lucretia Mott and Susan B. Anthony were other famous suffragettes.

Who gave his life to abolish slavery?

Abolitionists were people who wanted to abolish, or end, slavery in the U.S. In 1859, John Brown (1800–1859) made a plan to free slaves in the southern states. With 21 comrades, he captured an arsenal of weapons at Harpers Ferry, Virginia, where he tried, but failed, to incite a slave insurrection. He was captured by troops and hanged a few days later. He kept up his antislavery position throughout his trial.

Who had a dream?

Martin Luther King (1929–1968) was a Baptist clergyman and leader in the civil rights movement, which campaigned for equal rights for black Americans in the 1950s and 1960s. In 1963, he made a famous speech: "I have a dream," he said, "that my four little children will one day live in a nation where they will not be judged by the color of their skin, but by the content of their character." Martin Luther King was assassinated in Memphis, Tennessee, in 1968.

Martin Luther King vowed to use "passive resistance and the weapon of love" to fight prejudice.

Who founded thousands of libraries?

Andrew Carnegie (1835–1919) was an industrialist. Born in Scotland, he emigrated to the U.S. in 1848 and made a fortune in the steel business. With the money he made, he was able to build more than 2,800 public libraries worldwide.

Who was Jane Addams?

Jane Addams (1860–1935) was a social worker who fought against urban poverty in the U.S. In 1889, she founded a famous community center called Hull House in Chicago. She shared the Nobel Prize for Peace in 1931.

Who was the first American saint?

Elizabeth Ann Seton (1774–1821), who founded the Society for the Relief of Poor Widows with Small Children in 1797, and the Sisters of Charity in 1812. She was canonized (made a saint) in 1975.

Who was an angel in battle?

The American Red Cross in the U.S. was founded in 1881 by Clara Barton (1821–1912). She was its president until 1904. As a nurse during the Civil War, Clara Barton was known as the "angel of the battlefield."

Elizabeth Stanton (on the right) based her ideas on the Declaration of Independence. Susan Anthony stands beside her.

Who led the Apaches?

Cochise (1815–1874) led his Apache warriors against the U.S. Army in Arizona during the 1860s, after soldiers had killed his relatives. Cochise finally surrendered in 1872.

> Cochise's revenge for the deaths of his relatives was so effective that troops, settlers, and traders all left the region.

Who led the Confederates?

Thomas Jonathan Jackson (1824–1863) and Robert E. Lee (1807–1870). Their greatest victory against the Union was the Battle of Chancellorsville in May, 1863. At this battle, General "Stonewall" Jackson and General Lee, commander of the Army of Northern Virginia, defeated a larger Union side led by General Joe Hooker.

Who led the Union in the Civil War?

The two main military leaders were Ulysses S. Grant (1822–1885) and William Tecumseh Sherman (1820–1891). Grant won several battles before becoming commander-in-chief of all U.S. armies in 1864. Sherman campaigned in Georgia, splitting the Confederacy in two and depriving it of supplies.

Who was Paul Revere?

Paul Revere (1735–1818) was a folk hero of the American Revolution, which led to the United States gaining independence from Britain. After a career as a silversmith in Boston, Revere became a courier for the rebels. In 1775, he rode from Boston to Lexington to warn revolutionary leaders that British troops were on the way. This journey was made famous in a poem by Henry Longfellow called *Paul Revere's Ride.*

Which naval hero was killed in a duel?

Stephen Decatur (1779–1820), the naval officer who led a raid on Tripoli harbor, in Libya, in 1804 to destroy a captured U.S. ship. He was awarded the sword of honor. A fellow officer killed him in a duel.

Who is the U.S.S. *Nimitz* named after?

U.S.S. *Nimitz* is one of the largest aircraft carriers in the world. It is named after Admiral Chester William Nimitz (1885–1966), who served in submarines during World War I and was commander of U.S. naval forces in the Pacific in World War II.

Who said: "Damn the torpedoes!"?

David Glasgow Farragut (1801–1870). He was a naval captain on the Union side in the Civil War. In 1864, he sailed to Mobile Bay, Alabama, to capture the enemy's forts. Sailing through an area of mines (called torpedoes at the time), Farragut cried out: "Damn the torpedoes! Full speed ahead!"

Dwight Eisenhower became president in 1953 and remained in power for eight years.

Who led the U.S. in World War II?

Dwight D. Eisenhower (1890–1969) joined the army during World War I and served until 1948. In 1943, during World War II, he became a general and was given the title of Supreme Allied Commander. He was ordered to plan the Allied invasion of Europe, Operation Overlord, which began with the D-day landings in France on June 6, 1944.

Which racing driver became an air ace?

By 1914, Eddie Rickenbacker (1890–1973) was one of the top racing drivers in the U.S. He then joined the army, became an army pilot, and shot down 26 enemy planes during World War I. He eventually became president of Eastern Air Lines.

Who was the first person to find the North Pole?

Robert Edwin Peary (1856–1920), an explorer who made several expeditions to the Arctic around the turn of the century. On April 6, 1909, he became the first person to reach the North Pole.

Who made the first solo flight over the Atlantic Ocean?

Charles Lindburgh (1902–1974) made his flight in his aircraft *Spirit of St Louis* on May 20–21, 1927. The flight between New York and Paris, France, took 33 hours and 30 minutes. Lindburgh's main problem was how to stay awake.

Who made a giant leap for mankind?

On July 20, 1969, the lunar module *Apollo 11* landed on the Moon. Its commander Neil Alden Armstrong (born 1930) was the first man to step onto the Moon's surface, saying: "This is one small step for man, one giant leap for mankind." His fellow astronaut Buzz Aldrin followed him down the ladder to walk on the Moon.

Which around-the-world sailor could not swim?

Joshua Slocum (1844–1910), who spent most of his life at sea. In 1895, after retiring as a ship's captain, he set out in an old fishing boat named *Spray* to become the first man to sail around the world solo. But Slocum could not swim, and in 1910 he and *Spray* disappeared at sea.

Who disappeared while flying around the world?

The pioneering aviator Amelia Earhart (1897–1937). In 1932, she became the first woman to fly solo, nonstop, across the Atlantic, and to fly nonstop from coast to coast across the U.S. In 1937, she and copilot Frederick Noonan attempted to fly around the world, from Florida and back to California. Their aircraft disappeared after leaving New Guinea and was never found.

> Amelia's airplane is thought to have gone down off the coast of Howland Island, near Honolulu, Hawaii.

When *Apollo 11* landed on the Moon, the astronauts said: "The eagle has landed."

Who was the first American to fly around the Earth in space?

Lieutenant Colonel John Glenn made three orbits of the Earth in the *Friendship 7* capsule launched by the *Mercury–Atlas 6* spacecraft on February 20, 1962. The flight lasted nearly five hours.

Who led an expedition to the West?

The Lewis and Clark expedition set out in 1804 to explore the unknown lands to the west of the Mississippi River. In charge was Meriwether Lewis (1774–1809). The explorers returned nearly two and a half years later, having covered about 3,700 miles (5,950 km).

Which bird flew over the North Pole in 1924?

Richard Evelyn Byrd (1888–1957), a naval flier and explorer. In 1926, he became the first person to fly over the North Pole. Byrd also made five expeditions to the Antarctic and set up a U.S. Antarctic base.

Who helped found the American Geographical Society?

Adolphus Washington Greely (1844–1935). From 1881 to 1883, Greely carried out an exploration of Greenland. It ended in tragedy when all but six of his 25 men died of hunger during the winter.

Who flew around the world alone?

Wiley Post (1899–1935), a pilot who set many aviation records. In 1933, he flew around the world solo in a Lockheed Vega aircraft in just under eight days. Post was killed in a plane crash while piloting America's famous Will Rogers, who also died.

Who invented a cartoon mouse?

The man who started Disney films, Walter (Walt) Elias Disney (1901–1966). In 1928, Walt Disney invented the character Mickey Mouse and made the first Mickey Mouse movie, *Steamboat Willie*. Disney released *Snow White and the Seven Dwarfs*, the first feature-length animated movie, in 1937.

Disney's first theme park, Disneyland, opened in California in 1955.

Which magician escaped from everything?

Harry Houdini (1874–1926), real name Erik Weisz. Houdini became world famous as a magician and escapologist. His trademark trick was to escape from a sealed container full of water after being handcuffed and put in a straitjacket.

Which man with a girl's name played tough cowboys?

Marion Michael Morrison, better known as John Wayne (1907–1979), and often called simply "Duke," was famous for playing tough cowboys and soldiers in westerns and war films. He appeared in more than 150 feature films. His first major role was as the Ringo Kid in *Stagecoach* in 1939. He was presented with an Academy Award in 1969 for the part of Rooster Cogburn in *True Grit*.

What spectacular sort of show did Barnum run?

A circus. Phineas Taylor Barnum (1810–1891) was a showman who opened his own circus in 1871. Modestly, he named it, "The Greatest Show on Earth." In 1881, he joined forces with a rival to form the famous Barnum and Bailey Circus.

Who is America's most popular talk show host?

Oprah Winfrey (born 1954), who is known to most viewers simply as Oprah. She began her career as a news presenter for CBS at the age of 19. *The Oprah Winfrey Show* started in 1986.

Houdini was born in Hungary, but lived in the United States.

Who was Buffalo Bill?

Buffalo Bill's real name was William Frederick Cody (1846–1917). He was a scout for the U.S. army and a buffalo hunter. In 1883, he started Buffalo Bill's Wild West Show, which toured towns and cities across the U.S., with exhibitions of hunting, riding, and shooting.

Who are America's greatest actors?

Here are just a few:
Marlon Brando (1924–2004),
Humphrey Bogart (1899–1957),
Henry Fonda (1905–1982),
John Wayne (1907–1979),
Katherine Hepburn (1907–2003),
Bette Davis (1908–1989),
James Stewart (1908–1997),
Jane Fonda (born 1937),
Dustin Hoffman (born 1937),
Robert de Niro (born 1943),
Meryl Streep (born 1949),
Tom Hanks (born 1956),
and Michelle Pfeiffer (born 1957).

Which actress has won the most Oscars?

Katherine Hepburn (1907–2003) has won most Oscars in the Best Actress category, with four Academy Awards from 12 nominations. She was awarded her first for *Morning Glory* (1933) and her last for *On Golden Pond* (1981), when she was aged 74.

Who are the great American film directors?

A difficult question! Everybody will have their favorite. Some of the big names to look up are Frank Capra (1897–1991), Howard Hawks (1896–1977), John Ford (1895–1973), Stanley Kubrick (1928–1999), Francis Ford Coppola (born 1939), George Lucas (born 1944), and Steven Spielberg (born 1947).

Whose first success was *The Glass Menagerie?*

*T*he Glass Menagerie was written in 1945 by playwright Tennessee Williams (1911–1983). Williams wrote about the difficulties of life. Two other famous plays of his, *A Streetcar Named Desire* and *Cat on a Hot Tin Roof*, each won him a Pulitzer Prize.

Marlon Brando played the lead role in the film version of *A Streetcar Named Desire.*

Who created Huckleberry Finn?

Huckleberry Finn was a fictional character in the book entitled *The Adventures of Huckleberry Finn*, published in 1884. It was written by Mark Twain (1835–1910), one of the greatest writers in the U.S. Twain's real name was Samuel Longhorn Clemens. Before becoming a writer, Twain worked as a boat pilot on the Mississippi River. Two other famous novels of his are *The Prince and the Pauper* (1882) and *The Adventures of Tom Sawyer* (1876).

Who wrote the influential novel *Uncle Tom's Cabin?*

Uncle Tom's Cabin was the first antislavery novel to be published in the U.S. Written in 1852 by Harriet Beecher Stowe (1811–1896), it became a very popular book and play, and was influential in strengthening the antislavery cause before the Civil War.

Who was the first writer from the U.S. to win a Nobel Prize?

In 1930, Sinclair Lewis (1885–1951) became the first American to win a Nobel Prize for Literature. His novels address issues relating to women, race, and middle-class America, and include *Main Street, Babbitt,* and *Arrowsmith.*

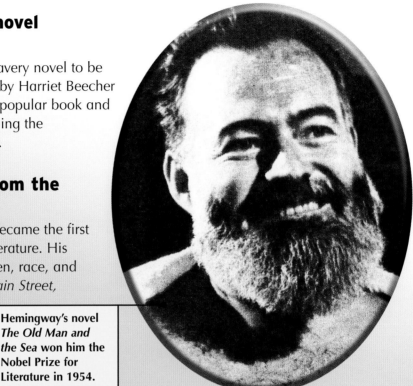

Hemingway's novel *The Old Man and the Sea* won him the Nobel Prize for Literature in 1954.

Whose most famous book is entitled *The Grapes of Wrath?*

John Steinbeck's (1902–1968). Written in 1939, it is a story about poor farmers living through a drought in the 1930s. The book won Steinbeck the Nobel Prize for Literature in 1962.

What did Ernest Hemingway write about?

Ernest Hemingway (1889–1961) was one of the greatest American writers. He wrote novels about brave people living dangerous lives, especially during wars. His titles include *A Farewell to Arms* (1929) and *For Whom the Bell Tolls* (1940).

Which writer demanded civil rights for blacks?

James Baldwin (1924–1987), a black American who wrote books, shorts stories, and plays about race relations in the U.S. In the 1950s, he campaigned for civil rights for blacks.

Who wrote the book *Little Women?*

Louisa May Alcott (1832–1888). She completed her most famous book, *Little Women,* in 1869, four years after the Civil War. Set in the 1800s, the book is about the lives of four sisters.

Which writer went with the wind?

Margaret Mitchell (1900–1949), who wrote only one novel: *Gone with the Wind.* The book took her 10 years to complete and became one of the most famous novels of all time. Its setting is Georgia during and after the Civil War, and the story is a love-hate romance between heroine Scarlett O'Hara and her admirer Rhett Butler. The book was published in 1936 and became an instant bestseller. In 1939, it was made into an even more famous film.

Who are America's greatest poets?

Difficult to say! Two of the best are Walt Whitman (1819–1892) and Henry Wadsworth Longfellow (1807–1882). Whitman was a Civil War nurse, whose poetry included war poems. Music was an important influence on his work. Longfellow was a popular poet who wrote *Paul Revere's Ride* and *Song of Hiawatha.*

Is Madonna her real name?

Yes, her full name is Madonna Louise Veronica Ritchie. She grew up in Pontiac, Michigan, a suburb of Detroit. Her father came to America from Italy and her mother was French-Canadian.

Which singer was known as "the King"?

"The King" was the nickname of the great rock and roll singer Elvis Presley (1935–1977). He was also known as "Elvis the Pelvis," because of the way he moved his hips while he sang. As a teenager, Presley lived in Memphis, Tennessee, where he listened to rhythm and blues music. This influenced his own new style of rock and roll, which brought him fame in the mid-1950s. Presley made 45 records, which sold more than 500 million copies. He also appeared in 33 films.

Which rock and roll singer died aged 22?

Buddy Holly (1936–1959), whose real name was Charles Harden Holly. A singer, songwriter, and guitarist, he made several hit records with his group The Crickets in the 1950s. He was killed in a plane crash.

Madonna is among the most photographed women in the world.

Who was Satchmo?

The jazz singer and trumpet player Louis Armstrong (1900–1971). Armstrong began singing in New Orleans as a teenager and became probably the most influential jazz musician of all time.

Who wrote the song *God Bless America*?

Russian-born songwriter Israel Baline (1888–1989), who moved to the United States as a boy. When his first song was published, the printer had misspelt his name Irving Berlin—a name the songwriter decided to adopt. Irving Berlin became perhaps the greatest songwriter in the U.S. He wrote more than 900 popular songs, including *God Bless America*, and dozens of Broadway musicals, including the popular hit show *Annie Get Your Gun*.

Who created the Jets and the Sharks?

Conductor and composer Leonard Bernstein (1918–1990). The Jets and the Sharks are the two New York City street gangs in the hugely popular musical *West Side Story*, which is based on Shakespeare's *Romeo and Juliet*.

Who composed military marches?

John Philip Sousa (1854–1932). Between 1880 and 1892, Sousa was leader of the band of the U.S. Marines. He wrote more than 100 tunes for military marches, including *The Stars and Stripes Forever*.

Which jazz player was called "Count"?

William "Count" Basie (1904–1984), but he was not a real count! The nickname was thought up by a radio station presenter. Basie was a top jazz pianist and band leader.

Who was America's greatest singer?

Many people would say the great Frank Sinatra. He started his singing career in the mid-1930s and was world famous by the early 1940s, when he also started acting. He won an Oscar in 1953 for his role in the film *From Here to Eternity*.

Which brothers wrote Broadway musicals?

George Gershwin (1898–1937) and Ira Gershwin (1896–1983). They teamed up to write several Broadway musicals, including *Porgy and Bess*. George composed the musical scores and Ira wrote the lyrics.

Frank Sinatra died in 1998 after a career spanning nearly 60 years.

Who painted soup cans?

The artist Andy Warhol (1928–1987). He was one of the leaders of a group of artists who started a new style of art called "pop art" in the early 1960s. The artists used everyday objects as subjects for their pictures. Warhol's most famous paintings are made up of lots of images of the same object, such as soup cans, painted in strong, vibrant colors.

Who designed a mile-high skyscraper?

Frank Lloyd Wright (1869–1959), a famous American architect who created extraordinary new styles of architecture. One of his most famous designs is the Guggenheim Museum in New York. Wright also designed many buildings that were never built, including a "mile-high" skyscraper, which would have been three times higher than the highest modern skyscrapers.

Who painted birds?

The ornithologist and artist John James Audubon (1785–1851). He made a detailed study of the native birds of the U.S., and in 1838 published *The Birds of America*, a book of paintings and drawings of America's birds!

Which artist painted in London ... at night?

James Whistler (1834–1903), who spent most of his working life outside the U.S. He moved to Paris, France, in 1855, and to London in 1859. During the 1870s, he painted several famous pictures of London, England, at night.

Western architecture is indebted to the important and influential designer, Frank Lloyd Wright.

Who is regarded as the first great American portrait painter?

John Singleton Copley (1738–1815), considered by many to be the greatest portrait painter of his time. He worked in Boston, New York City, Philadelphia, and London, England. His portraits include those of revolutionary hero Paul Revere and politician Samuel Adams, a signatory of the Declaration of Independence.

Who is famous for sculpting people?

Poor eyesight prevented Sir Jacob Epstein (1880–1959) becoming a painter. Instead he turned to sculpting and became brilliant at creating figures of people. Epstein was born in New York City, but moved to England; he set up a studio in London in 1905.

What did Buckminster Fuller invent?

Buckminster Fuller (1895–1983) was an architect and engineer who came up with several new ideas for building shapes. One of these was the geodesic dome—a domed building made from a framework of triangles.

Who is famous for dripping paint?

Artist Jackson Pollock (1912–1956), who painted abstract pictures expressive of his feelings. He often used the technique of dripping and swirling lines of paint on to a huge canvas—a technique he called "action painting."

What did Ansel Adams do?

Ansel Adams (1902–1984) was a photographer. He took superb black-and-white photographs of landscapes, especially of the southwest and west of the U.S. He also wrote many books on photographic technique.

Andy Warhol was not just an artist; he was also involved in film-making, photography, and publishing.

Who produced a Model-T?

The Model-T was the first mass-produced car. It was made by the Ford Motor Company, which was started in 1903 by Henry Ford (1863–1947). More than 15 million Model-Ts were made and sold.

Who started a detective agency?

Allan Pinkerton (1819–1884). He was in charge of army spies on the Union side during the Civil War. In 1850, he started a private detective agency in Chicago, which became the famous Pinkerton National Detective Agency.

Who got rich by keeping others warm?

John Jacob Astor (1763–1848). Born in Germany, he emigrated to the U.S. with no money. He started his career in a small shop in New York City selling furs, and in time built up the American Fur Company, which eventually made him the richest man in the U.S.

Who got rich by staying cold?

Clarence Birdseye (1886–1956), an inventor who started the frozen food industry. One of his experiments was to try to keep food fresh for long periods by freezing it. The freezing process he developed kept the flavor of the food while it was frozen.

The Model-T was known as "the motor car for the multitude."

Who encouraged education?

Nicholas Murray Butler (1862–1947)—joint winner of the Nobel Prize for Peace in 1931—was one of America's leading educationalists. Another was John Dewey (1859–1952), who gave lectures on education all over the world.

Who got rich by sending people to sleep?

In 1859, George Mortimer Pullman (1831–1897) started up a business converting regular railroad cars into luxury sleeping cars. His Pullmans Palace Car Company made him a fortune, which he used to build a town, now part of Chicago. "Pullman" is now used to describe any luxury railroad carriage.

Who worked out that $E=mc^2$?

A man with one of the greatest scientific minds of all time, Albert Einstein (1879–1955). Einstein was a theoretical physicist. He was born in Germany, moved to the United States in 1933, and became an American citizen in 1940. His most famous works are his *Special Theory of Relativity* (1905) and *General Theory of Relativity* (1916). Part of the *Special Theory* stated that mass (m) can be changed into energy (E) according to the equation $E=mc^2$.

Who made a fortune from software?

Businessman Bill Gates (born 1955). He founded Microsoft, the company which created the operating systems MS-DOS and Windows. These computer programs are now used on almost every PC in the world. Gates left university early to start Microsoft with a friend, and became a billionaire in 1986, when the company was successfully floated on the stock market.

From the age of 12, Einstein was determined to solve "the riddle of the world."

Who has a telescope named after him?

Who was a famous brain surgeon?

Harvey Williams Cushing (1869–1939). He was the first person to describe the medical disorder that is now called Cushing's syndrome.

Edwin Powell Hubble (1889–1953), the famous astronomer who was the first person to show that the universe is made up of huge groups of stars called galaxies with space between them. Hubble also showed that the universe is getting bigger and bigger. He did most of his work at Mount Wilson Observatory, California. The Hubble Space Telescope that orbits the Earth is named after him.

Who helped to build a nuclear bomb?

In 1942, nuclear scientist Robert J. Oppenheimer (1904–1967) became director of the Los Alamos laboratory in New Mexico. Here scientists created the world's first atomic bomb.

Who is the only man to win two Nobel prizes?

Linus Carl Pauling (1901–1994) was a brilliant chemist. He was awarded his first Nobel Prize (for Chemistry) in 1954. In 1962, Pauling was awarded the Nobel Prize for Peace for his campaign against nuclear weapons testing.

Pauling was the man who found the cause of the disease, sickle cell anemia.

Who modeled DNA?

DNA is a chemical inside cells that holds the code for how all animals and plants grow and live. The way the chemical's atoms are joined together was first modeled in 1953 by biologist James Dewey Watson (1928–2004) from the United States and British scientist Francis Crick (born 1916).

What did Albert Michelson measure?

The speed of light. Albert Michelson (1852–1931) was a physicist who built a device called an interferometer, which he used to measure the speed of light far more accurately than it had been measured before. In 1907, he received the Nobel Prize for Physics.

Who discovered Barnard's Star?

No surprise here! It was the astronomer Edward Emerson Barnard (1857–1923). In 1916, Barnard discovered a star that was moving very quickly compared to the other stars. It is now called Barnard's Star. Barnard also discovered 16 comets and a moon of Jupiter.

Who was the first woman to become a doctor?

Elizabeth Blackwell (1821–1910) was born in England but moved to the U.S. in 1832. In 1849 she graduated from Geneva Medical College, New York, to become the first woman in the U.S. to get a medical degree.

Edwin Hubble originally studied law, but changed course to study astronomy. He became one of the finest astronomers of the modern age.

Who invented a famous code?

Samuel Finley Breese Morse (1791–1872). Morse was an inventor and pioneer of the electric telegraph—a device for sending messages along wires. He invented a code (known as Morse code) composed of groups of dots and dashes that represent letters and numbers.

The first name for the telephone was the "electrical speech machine."

Who said: "Mr. Watson, come here"?

The inventor of the telephone, Alexander Graham Bell (1847–1922). Bell was born in Scotland. He was interested in speech therapy, which he taught at a school in Boston. In 1876, he demonstrated an invention that allowed speech to be sent along a wire—the telephone. His first words on his telephone were: "Mr. Watson, come here," spoken to his assistant in the next room.

Who made rubber useful?

A process named vulcanization makes rubber last longer and makes it stay rubbery when it is very hot or very cold. The process was invented by Charles Goodyear (1800–1860) in 1839, and it allowed long-lasting vehicle tires to be made.

What did Chester Floyd Carlson copy?

Anything written on paper—he invented xerography (now called photocopying) in 1938. Chester Floyd Carlson (1906–1968) founded a company that is now the Xerox Corporation.

Who helped us to take holiday snaps?

George Eastman (1854–1932), a pioneer of photography. In 1888, he developed the first simple camera that was sold to the public, the Kodak camera. It was loaded with film that the owner could send off for processing.

How did Robert Hutchings Goddard rocket to fame?

He was a builder of rockets. In 1926, Robert Hutchings Goddard (1882–1945) developed the first rocket fueled by liquids rather than solid fuel.

Who got the sewing machine going?

The sewing machine was actually invented in England in 1790 by Thomas Saint. But it was American Isaac Merritt Singer (1811–1875) who made it popular. He marketed the first sewing machine for home use (patented in 1851). The Singer became a worldwide best seller.

Which brothers built the first airplane?

The Wright brothers: Orville (1871–1948) and Wilbur (1867–1912). In December 1903, at Kitty Hawk, North Carolina, their home-built plane made the first controlled flight by a powered aircraft.

Edison founded the Edison Electric Light Company in 1878.

Which telegraph operator invented light bulbs?

Thomas Alva Edison (1847–1931), probably the greatest inventor of all time. While working as a telegraph operator on the railroads during the 1860s, he got the idea for a new type of telegraph machine. In 1879, he invented the first practical incandescent light bulb (one that produced white heat), which could be used in the home. He also invented the phonograph, for recording sound.

Who made elevators safe?

In 1852, Elisha Graves Otis (1811–1861) invented a safety device that stopped goods' elevators falling to the ground if the rope broke. This allowed safe passenger elevators to be developed.

Who is "Magic" on a basketball court?

The basketball player Earvin "Magic" Johnson (born 1959). For the Los Angeles Lakers, Johnson was MVP (Most Valuable Player) three times, helping them win five NBA titles. He played in the U.S. Dream Team at the 1992 Olympics, despite being diagnosed HIV positive in 1991.

Who ran to fame in 1936?

The sprinter Jesse Owens (1913–1980). Owens' real name was James Cleveland, but his school teacher turned his initials, JC, into Jesse! At 22, he set four world sprinting and jumping records in the space of 45 minutes. At the 1936 Olympics in Berlin, Owens won four gold medals— for the 100 meters, the 200 meters, the long jump, and the sprint relay.

Which tennis tournament has Pete Sampras not won?

Despite his great career success, Sampras never got further than the semifinals in the French Open (in 2002). The games at the Open are played on red clay courts, which Sampras is said not to enjoy playing on. He sees the Open as a major challenge.

Peter Sampras is rated one of the best tennis players in the world.

Who was named Golfer of the Century?

In 1988, the Professional Golf Association of the United States named Jack Nicklaus (born 1940) Golfer of the Century. He became a professional golfer in 1961, and a year later became the youngest player to win the U.S. Open, the first of his 20 championship wins.

Who is the greatest quarterback?

Joe Montana (born 1956) dominated the NFL (National Football League) during the 1980s playing for the San Francisco 49ers. With Montana in command, they won the Super Bowl four times, three times with Montana as MVP (Most Valuable Player).

Who was the greatest all-around athlete?

At the 1912 Stockholm Olympics in Sweden, Jim Thorpe (1888–1953) won both the pentathlon and decathlon. The King of Sweden said to him: "Sir, you are the greatest athlete in the world." Thorpe also played professional baseball and football.

What is The House that Ruth Built?

Yankee Stadium, home of the New York Yankees baseball team. It got its nickname from Babe Ruth (1895–1948), the greatest baseball batter of all time, who played in it throughout the 1920s. He hit a record 714 home runs in his career.

Who swam to seven Olympic golds?

At the 1972 Olympics in Munich, Germany, U.S. swimmer Mark Spitz (born 1950) made history by winning seven gold medals, four in individual events and three in relays.

Who started life as Cassius Clay?

The heavyweight boxer Muhammad Ali (born 1942). He was born as Cassius Clay, but changed his name in 1964 after becoming a Muslim. Ali was the only boxer to win the heavyweight world championship three times, in 1964, 1974, and 1978. He won 56 of his 61 professional fights. Ali proclaimed himself "The Greatest," and made up raplike poems about himself.

"Magic" Johnson gives a lot of money to charities supporting education and youth.

Who were the Jackson Five?

A singing group, made up of five sons of the Jackson family. They made records on the famous Motown label. The member of the group to win most fame as a singer was Michael Jackson.

What did the Kennedy brothers do?

Joseph Patrick Kennedy (1888–1969) was the father of three sons, who became America's most famous political family. John Fitzgerald Kennedy (1917–1963) was inaugurated as president in 1961, and assassinated in 1963. Robert Francis Kennedy (1925–1968) was attorney general. Like his brother, he was also assassinated; the killing took place in 1968, while he was running for president. Edward Moore Kennedy (born 1932) is a senator.

What were the names of the Marx brothers?

The Marx brothers were a zany comedy team who performed on stage and in films, such as *A Night at the Opera*. The main members of the team were Groucho (1890–1977), Harpo (1888–1964), and Chico (1887–1961).

Who founded their own museum?

The Guggenheims, a family of industrialists. Meyer Guggenheim (1828–1905) emigrated from Switzerland in 1847 and had seven sons. One of the seven, Simon Guggenheim (1867–1941), started a foundation that helped artists and writers. Another, Solomon Robert Guggenheim (1861–1949), started a foundation that built the famous Guggenheim Museum in New York City.

How did Laurel meet Hardy?

Stan Laurel (1890–1965) and Oliver Hardy (1892–1957) were a comedy duo who made more than 200 films, almost 90 of which were slapstick. The two men joined a film studio separately in 1926, and the studio owner persuaded them to team up.

How were the two President Roosevelts related?

Theodore Roosevelt (1858–1919), the 26th president, was a fifth cousin of Franklin D. Roosevelt (1882–1945), the 32nd president.

The first Jackson Five single in 1970 was *I Want You Back*. It sold two million copies.

What did Rodgers and Hammerstein write?

Oscar Hammerstein (1895–1960) wrote the lyrics to many musicals, and often teamed up with the composer Richard Rodgers (1902–1981). Together they created famous musicals such as *Oklahoma!* and *The King and I*.

What did the Maxim family make?

Guns and ammunition. Sir Hiram Stevens Maxim (1840–1916) invented the Maxim machine gun, which was the first fully automatic machine gun. His brother Hudson Maxim (1853–1927) developed high explosives, and his son Hiram Percy Maxim (1869–1936) invented the silencer.

THE 50 STATES

1. In which state is Crater Lake National Park?
2. What is one of Montana's nicknames?
3. Where did Custer's Last Stand take place?
4. In which state is America's highest mountain?
5. Which state is famous for making cheese?
6. Which state has the lowest rainfall?
7. Which strange monster can you meet in Arizona?
8. Who did the Texans fight at the Alamo?
9. Which state is famous for its red chickens?
10. In which state is Harvard University?
11. Which "King" lived in Memphis, Tennessee?
12. Which is the only state to produce diamonds?

1. Oregon 2. Big Sky Country, Land of the Shining Mountains, the Treasure State or Bonanza State 3. Little Big Horn, South Dakota 4. Alaska 5. Wisconsin 6. Nevada 7. The Gila monster 8. The Mexicans 9. Rhode Island 10. Massachusetts 11. Elvis Presley 12. Arkansas

NATIVE AMERICANS

1. The American Constitution was based on which Native American elected council of the late 15th century?
2. What does "Sioux" mean?
3. From where did the Apache originate?
4. Who built "apartment blocks" in the canyons of Arizona and New Mexico?
5. What would 15 eagle feathers get you in 1850?
6. What were porcupine hairs and sticks used for?
7. What are moccasins?
8. What was a Native American baby carried in?
9. Who was made to walk the Trail of Tears?
10. What were Mohawks not afraid of?

1. The Iroquois Confederacy 2. "Snake" or "enemies to the west" 3. Canada 4. The Anasazi 5. A valuable horse 6. Brushing teeth 7. Shoes 8. A papoose 9. The Cherokees 10. Heights

PILGRIMS

1. Who lived in longhouses?
2. Who sketched Native American scenes?
3. Who did John Rolfe marry?
4. What is the name of the ship that carried the Pilgrims to America?
5. What year did the *Mayflower* leave Plymouth, England?
6. When was the first Thanksgiving?
7. Which Wampanoag chief befriended the Pilgrims?
8. Who was Maryland named after?
9. What was King Philip's real name?
10. What happened on July 4, 1776?

1. The Iroquois 2. John White 3. Pocahontas 4. The *Mayflower* 5. 1620 6. The fall of 1621 7. Massasoit 8. The Virgin Mary 9. Metacomet 10. The Declaration of Independence was signed

HOW THE WEST WAS WON

1. What is the name for the tentlike home in which some Native Americans live?
2. What did the Pacific coast tribes use instead of money?
3. What did the Spanish Conquistadors believe they would find in the Americas?
4. Who sent Lewis and Clark on an expedition?
5. Which area of land did President Jefferson buy for $15 million?
6. Of which Church was Brigham Young the head?
7. Which disease caused many deaths on the Oregon and California trails?
8. Which president had to prove to his government that there was gold in the hills?
9. Who invented jeans?
10. What did the Union Pacific and the Central Pacific companies build?
11. Where did the "Wild Bunch" hang out?

1. A tepee 2. Shells 3. Gold 4. President Thomas Jefferson 5. Louisiana 6. The Mormons 7. Cholera 8. President Polk 9. Levi Strauss 10. A railroad that linked the east and west coasts of America 11. At the Hole in the Wall, a gorge in Wyoming

THE CIVIL WAR

1. Which state had two presidents?
2. What was Harriet Tubman's nickname?
3. Which famous president was very tall?
4. Which side sang *Yankee Doodle*?
5. What were used to spy on the enemy from above?
6. What was an ironclad?
7. What was the nickname of the North's naval blockade of the South?
8. Who was nicknamed "Stonewall"?
9. Who won the Battle of Gettysburg?
10. Which woman helped the wounded on the battlefields?
11. In which year did slavery officially end?

1. Kentucky 2. Moses 3. Abraham Lincoln 4. The North
5. Hot air balloons 6. An armored ship 7. Scott's Anaconda Plan
8. General Thomas J. Jackson 9. The North 10. Clara Barton 11. 1863

PRESIDENTS

1. Where is the Oval Office?
2. What is the name of the president's 'plane?
3. Which president was never elected?
4. How old was Ronald Reagan when he was inaugurated?
5. What does CIA stand for?
6. Which Olympics did Jimmy Carter order a boycott of?
7. Who did Lee Harvey Oswald shoot?
8. Who did Jack Ruby shoot?
9. What medal did John F. Kennedy win?
10. Which president received a dog as a present?
11. Where are the greatest American presidents' heads carved into rock?

1. The White House 2. Air Force One 3. Gerald Ford 4. 69 5. Central Intelligence Agency
6. 1980 Moscow Olympics 7. John F. Kennedy 8. Lee Harvey Oswald 9. The Purple Heart
10. Richard Nixon 11. Mount Rushmore

SPORTING HEROES

1. What did Walter Camp invent?
2. Which sport has the Queensberry Rules?
3. What golfing championship started in 1895?
4. What was Gentleman Jim's real name?
5. Who was the first black professional American football player?
6. In 1935, who set three world records in about 45 minutes?
7. Who was married to Joe DiMaggio?
8. Who said: "Float like a butterfly, sting like a bee"?
9. What is Jack Nicklaus' nickname?
10. Which tennis star was engaged to Chris Evert?
11. What nationality is Martina Navratilova?

1. American football 2. Boxing 3. The U.S. Open 4. Jim Corbett 5. Charles Follis 6. Jesse Owens 7. Marilyn Monroe 8. Muhammad Ali 9. Golden Bear 10. Jimmy Connors 11. American

GREAT AMERICANS

1. What did Andrew Carnegie build?
2. Which Baptist clergyman led the civil rights movement in the 1960s?
3. Who is Billy Graham?
4. What year did U.S. astronauts first step onto the Moon?
5. What was William Frederick Cody's other name?
6. Who wrote *A Farewell to Arms*?
7. What instrument did Satchmo play?
8. Which rock and roll singer was killed in a 'plane crash?
9. Who started Microsoft?
10. Who invented the telephone?
11. Who is Cassius Clay?

1. Libraries 2. Martin Luther King 3. An evangelist preacher 4. 1969 5. Buffalo Bill 6. Ernest Hemingway 7. The trumpet 8. Buddy Holly 9. Bill Gates 10. Alexander Graham Bell 11. Muhammad Ali

Index

A

Abdul-Jabbar, K. 183
abolitionists 116, 117, 121, 136
Acoma 20, 91
Adams, A. 205
Adams, J. 140, 142, 143, 156, 157, 158
Adams, J.Q. 142, 158, 163
Adams S. 205
Addams, J. 193
Agnew, S. 142
Air Force One 141, 151
Alabama 126
Alabama 9, 33, 114
Alamo 14, 20, 21
Alaska 8, 9, 13, 53
Alcatraz 18
Alcindor, L. 183
Alcott, L.M. 135, 201
Aldrin, B. 196
Algonquian 47, 49, 67
Ali, M. 180, 181, 182, 187, 188, 213
American Indian Movement 60
American Revolution 25, 27, 148
Amos, R. 171
Anasazi 43
Andersonville prison 132, 133
Anne 79
Anson, A.C. 168
Anthony, S. 193
Antietam Creek 129
Apache 41, 47, 48, 58, 59, 61, 93
Apalachee 48
Appalachian Mountains 87, 91, 115
Arapaho 54
Arbor Day 23
Arizona 8, 20, 21, 39, 43, 59, 61, 109

Arkansas 9, 30, 31, 114
Armstrong, L. 203
Armstrong, N.A. 196
Army Medical Museum 131
Arthur, C. 142
Ashe, A. 183
Astor, J.J. 206
Attorney General 146, 159
Audubon, J.J. 204

B

backwoodsmen 86
Baldwin, J. 201
Balloon Corps 125
Barnard, E.E. 209
Barnum, P.T. 198
Barton, C. 135, 193
baseball 137, 166, 167, 168, 169, 170–171, 172–173, 174–175, 176, 177, 178, 179, 189
Basie, W. 203
basketball 167, 170, 176, 183, 185, 186, 187
battles 115, 120, 121, 122, 125, 126, 128–129, 131, 133, 134, 135, 137
Bay of Pigs 151
Bell, A.G. 210
Berlin, I. 203
Bernstein, L. 203
Billy the Kid 20, 108
Birdseye, C. 206
Black Hills 111
Blackfeet 50, 55
Blackwell, E. 209
Blaine, J. 156
blockades 115, 127
Bogart, H. 199
Boone, D. 87
Boonesborough 87
Booth, J.W. 136, 137, 153
border ruffians 116
Boston 80, 81
Boston Tea Party 27
Bouvier, J. 158
boxing 167, 169, 171, 177, 180, 182, 187

Boyd, B. 125
Braddock, J. 177
Bradford, W. 69, 70, 78
Brady, M.B. 125
Brains Trust 157
Brando, M. 199, 200
Brewster, W. 69
Brezhnev, L. 147
Britain 127
broncos 102
Brown, J. 28, 117, 119, 120, 136, 183, 188, 192
Buchanan, J. 142, 149
buffalo 41, 42, 44, 45, 46, 47, 48, 58, 90, 93, 96, 107, 110, 111
Buffalo Calf Road Woman 55
Bull Run 128–129
Bunker Hill 85
burial mounds 38, 53
Burns, T. 173
Bush, G. 142, 143, 151, 155, 160
Bush G.W. 142
Butler, General 123
Butler, N.M. 207
Byrd, R.E. 197
Babe Ruth 213

C

Cabot, J. 64, 65
Calamity Jane 12
California 8, 9, 17, 18, 19, 53, 90, 100, 101, 103, 104, 105, 106, 107, 115
Camp, W. 166, 167
Cape Cod 70, 72
Capra, F. 199
Carlson, C.F. 210
Carnegie, A. 193
carpetbaggers 137
Carson, K. 55
Carter, J. 142, 147, 151
Cartier J. 65
Cartwright, A. 166, 169
Carver, J. 73, 75
Cascade Mountains 11, 90, 100
Cassidy, B. 109

casualties 115, 122, 135
Catlin, G. 58
cattle 102, 103, 108, 109
Central Intelligence Agency (CIA) 147, 151, 160
Central Pacific 106, 107
Champlain, S. de 65
Cherokee 23, 28, 40, 44, 48, 55, 56, 57, 58, 87
Chesapeake 65
Cheyenne 54, 55
Chickasaws 23
Chicksaw 40, 49
Chief Joseph 55
Chief Looking Glass 57
children 68, 69, 70, 80, 101, 111
China 106
Chinook 90
Chippewa 41
Chiricahua 59
Chisholm Trail 102
Choctaw 23, 40, 43, 44, 48, 49
Civil War 24, 28, 33, 146, 148, 149, 153, 154, 160
Clark, D. 185
Clark, W. 11, 41, 91, 94–95, 96, 97, 197
Clatsop 90, 97
Clay, C. 180, 213
Clem, J. 123
Cleveland, G. 142, 145, 156
Clinton, W.J. (Bill) 61, 142, 144
Cobb, T. 176
Cochise 59, 194
Cody, W.F. 17, 199
Cold War 147, 151, 154
Colorado 8, 16, 17, 115
Columbia River 10, 11, 90, 97, 100
Columbus, C. 38, 39, 64
communications 125
Confederacy 20, 24, 114, 120, 121, 146, 148
Confederates 24, 114, 115, 117, 118, 119, 120, 121, 123, 124, 125,